WHITGIFT

and

The English Church

is one of the volumes
in the

TEACH YOURSELF HISTORY
LIBRARY

Edited by A. L. ROWSE

Teach Yourself History

VOLUMES READY OR IN PREPARATION

WHITGIFT

and

The English Church

by

V. J. K. BROOK

*Chaplain and Fellow of All Souls College; formerly
Censor of St. Catherine's Society, Oxford.*

THE ENGLISH UNIVERSITIES PRESS LTD
102, Newgate Street
LONDON, E.C.1

FIRST PRINTED   1957

PRINTED AND BOUND IN ENGLAND
FOR THE ENGLISH UNIVERSITIES PRESS, LTD.,
BY HAZELL WATSON AND VINEY LTD., AYLESBURY

Contents

A General Introduction
to the Series

THIS series has been undertaken in the conviction
that there can be no subject of study more important than history. Great as have been the conquests of
natural science in our time—such that many think of
ours as a scientific age *par excellence*—it is even more
urgent and necessary that advances should be made in
the social sciences, if we are to gain control of the forces
of nature loosed upon us. The bed out of which all the
social sciences spring is history; there they find, in
greater or lesser degree, subject-matter and material,
verification or contradiction.

There is no end to what we can learn from history,
if only we will, for it is coterminous with life. Its special
field is the life of man in society, and at every point we
can learn vicariously from the experience of others before us in history.

To make one point only—the understanding of politics : how can we hope to understand the world of
affairs around us if we do not know how it came to be
what it is? How to understand Germany, or Soviet
Russia or the United States—or ourselves, without
knowing something of their history?

There is no subject that is more useful, or indeed in-
dispensable.

Some evidence of the growing awareness of this
may be seen in the immense increase in the interest of
the reading public in history, and the much larger
place the subject has come to take in education in our
time.

This series has been planned to meet the needs and demands of a very wide public and of education—they are indeed the same. I am convinced that the most congenial, as well as the most concrete and practical, approach to history is the biographical, through the lives of the great men whose actions have been so much part of history, and whose careers in turn have been so moulded and formed by events.

The key idea of this series, and what distinguishes it from any other that has appeared, is the intention by way of a biography of a great man to open up a significant historical theme; for example, Cromwell and the Puritan Revolution, or Lenin and the Russian Revolution.

My hope is, in the end, as the series fills out and completes itself, by a sufficient number of biographies to cover whole periods and subjects in that way. To give you the history of the United States, for example, or the British Empire or France, *via* a number of biographies of their leading historical figures.

That should be something new, as well as convenient and practical, in education.

I need hardly say that I am a strong believer in people with good academic standards writing once more for the general reading public, and of the public being given the best that the universities can provide. From this point of view this series is intended to bring the University into the homes of the people.

A. L. ROWSE.

ALL SOULS COLLEGE,
    OXFORD.

Chapter One

Early Life of Whitgift

JOHN WHITGIFT was born in 1530 at Grimsby: he died in 1604. His life, therefore, exactly covers the vital years in which the Church in England first of all broke away from obedience to Rome and was then "established" or stabilised ("stabilita" is the word in the Latin canons, not "fundata") under Elizabeth.

His family was, it seems, prosperous. His grandfather was a Yorkshire gentleman who had many children, some of whom he "made scholars", while he settled others in various courses of life. Henry, the father of John, was a merchant in Grimsby in comfortable circumstances; one of Henry's brothers, Robert—presumably one of the scholars—was Abbot of Wellow, near Grimsby. He was an important influence in the life of his nephew, for he much concerned himself with the education of boys and took John into his care. There is no evidence that Robert ever severed his ties with the old beliefs; but he was clearly disturbed in mind, and outspoken. Later on John often remembered that he had said that their religion could not long continue, for he had read the Scriptures over and over and could never find therein that it was founded by God. The remark evidently made a deep impression and was recalled by John with pleasure.

As the boy showed much promise, Robert sent him after a time to London to a good school, St. Anthony's, where both Sir Thomas More and Archbishop Heath had been pupils. He was put to live with an aunt, a devout woman, wife to one of the vergers at St. Paul's. In the later years of Henry VIII, his surroundings could scarcely have been more conservative. But even at this early date he began to show the firm self-reliance which was to be clear in his later life. Whether it was due to his uncle's doubts, or whether in London he had come into touch with more advanced views is unknown; what is certain is that he shocked his aunt by his refusal to attend "morrow mass" with her, even resisting the persuasion of some of the canons of the cathedral whom she procured to talk to him. In the end, she thrust him from her doors, attributing to his presence some domestic misfortunes which had befallen her. Her parting shot was that whereas, at first, she thought she was entertaining a saint, she now perceived that he was a devil!

He returned to Grimsby, but his parents, impressed by his advance in learning, and guided by the advice of Robert, sent him to Cambridge, apparently at their own cost, about 1548 or 1549. At first he was at Queens', but he soon transferred to Pembroke, which he seems to have joined in May 1550. The move was significant. The Master was Ridley who, though now a Bishop, doubtless still maintained a strong hold and influence on the college; the President was Grindal. One of the Fellows was Bradford, converted in middle life and already a noted upholder of reforming views. It is not reasonable to doubt that Whitgift was drawn to Pembroke by what he knew of the tone and atmosphere of the college. For a time Bradford, whose almost fanatical zeal was tempered by great kindliness in personal relations, was his tutor. His outspoken honesty, the rigid discipline of his life, largely given to prayer and meditation, his real humility, can scarcely have failed to confirm a young man such as Whitgift in the views he was now favouring. Equally, he himself made a good impression on the college authorities. About now his father suffered serious losses at sea and there were financial difficulties. Ridley thereupon, advised by Bradford of the circumstances and promise of the young man, appointed him to a bible-clerkship in the college. Thus enabled to remain in Cambridge, he took his B.A. in 1553-4. In 1555 he was elected a Fellow of Peterhouse.

The Master, Andrew Perne, though later on a byword among puritans for his easy accommodation to whatever views prevailed in successive governments, proved a very staunch friend to Whitgift and earned his life-long affection. When Whitgift fell seriously ill, Perne visited him personally, charged the woman to whose house he had been removed to see that he lacked nothing, guaranteeing that all expenses would be met, if need be, from his own pocket. Later on, when the Marian Visitors were in Cambridge, it was Perne who advised him not to be "troublesome in uttering his opinion", promising that he himself would "wink" at him. Whitgift was thus saved from having to go abroad, as he had thought of doing, and was able to carry on with his work, laying the foundations of the massive knowledge which on occasion he was able to display in his writings. He took his M.A. in 1557, and proceeded with work for the B.D. which he took in 1563. It is certainly not fanciful to suggest that all this had an important bearing on his subsequent life. Few of his contemporaries who went abroad failed to be deeply impressed by the models of a reformed church in full working order which they found at Zurich or Geneva. Instead of experiencing the influence of such direct contact, Whitgift was quietly busy with his studies. He was not unconscious of his debt to Perne who, when Whitgift was Archbishop, was a frequent visitor at Lambeth where, indeed, he died.

From his cautious obscurity Whitgift quickly emerged to a position of influence under Queen Elizabeth. Ordained in 1560, he seems almost at once, by a sermon at St. Mary's, to have won approbation—

especially among "the chief of the University". It is typical that, even in his first public pronouncement, he should thus clearly have shown his sympathies. Cox, the Bishop of Ely, strongly anti-Roman, a stout upholder of authority and order, appointed him one of his chaplains and collated him to the rectory of Teversham. In 1563 he was elected Lady Margaret Lecturer in Divinity, a striking proof of the impression he had made in so short a time. His lectures on the Epistle to the Hebrews and the Apocalypse were so acceptable that, in 1566, the University voted an increase in the emoluments of the lectureship.

Having now an established position in the University, he began to show what was to be his life-long interest in and capacity for administration and orderly government. Under the University statutes the Regent Masters (that is, on the whole, the junior M.A.s who were still under obligation to teach) had great power in the choosing of the Vice-Chancellor and other University officers. They were using it with a good deal of faction and unseemliness to override the authority of the Heads of colleges. A number of the latter, headed by the Vice-Chancellor, wrote to the Chancellor in 1564 to ask him to promote new arrangements for elections which would give the real control to the Heads and so "bridle the untamed affections of young Regents". Despite his youth, Whitgift sided with the Heads : his signature was, indeed, the only one not of a Head, with one possible exception. The fact illustrates alike his own leanings and the weight which the authorities already attached to his support. Similarly, in the next year he joined the Vice-Chancellor and three other Heads in a letter to Cecil, their Chancellor, to urge him to use his influence with the Queen to prevent a rigid Order being imposed on the University for the wearing of the traditional dress, including, especially, the surplice. They urged that there were many pious and learned men who in conscience thought such

garments unlawful and who, if they were strictly enjoined, would have no choice but to leave the University, to the serious injury both of the preaching of
the gospel and of good learning. The letter was not
well received : it was against the Queen's policy. The
Vice-Chancellor was seriously rebuked for it, and the
wearing of clerical attire was firmly ordered.

Once the Order was made, Whitgift loyally supported it, and regularly in the University pulpit answered those who spoke against it. The explanation is
not to be found in servility, as he himself shows. On the
basis of the letter he was subsequently accused to Cecil
of non-conformity, a charge he strongly denied : "I
never encouraged any to withstand the Queen's Majes-
ties laws in that behalf; but I both have and do, by all
means I may, seek to persuade men to conform themselves. For it grieveth me that any man should cease
from preaching for the use of those things, being of
themselves indifferent." His sympathetic attempt to
spare men whose scruples he did not share, or even
think important, was at least as characteristic as his insistence on keeping the law once it was declared,
though he had not wished for it.

Even when full allowance is made for the position
which Whitgift had by now evidently won in Cambridge, his advancements in 1567 are astonishing. In
that year he took his D.D., the title of his exercise being
that "The Pope is that Antichrist". In April he was recalled to his old college, Pembroke, to be Master in
place of Hutton, nominated to the Deanery of York.
His former patron Grindal, himself lately Master there,
urged the choice and the college cordially agreed. He
was also chosen to succeed Hutton as Queen's Professor of Divinity. Nor was that the end. In this year he
was chosen to preach before the Queen who, with her
almost infallible instinct in the choice of her agents,
was at once struck by his quality and declared that he

"had a white-gift indeed". On her nomination (no doubt in part influenced by Cecil and Bacon who both knew and approved of him) he was in July made Master of the royal foundation of Trinity College.

It was in connection with this appointment that he wrote his letter to Cecil to defend himself against the charge of non-conformity. But the letter is further interesting in its explanation of his eagerness—for he was eager—to be appointed to Trinity. The college had not then the eminence it now has (and, indeed, has enjoyed ever since Whitgift's Mastership). It seems odd that he should wish to go there from Pembroke, where he was at home and was plainly popular. The explanation, once given, is simple, though, to a modern reader, startling. He could not afford to remain as Master of Pembroke. The Mastership was only worth four pounds a year, and eighteen-pence a week for commons. The main part of his income came from his professorship, but even so he was in debt, not through prodigality, but through extreme necessity, and saw no prospect of clearing himself. It is only fair to Whitgift to record this. He was not an ambitious man, insensible to the emotion of gratitude; his endowment of a bible-clerkship at Peterhouse while he was still a Fellow there, no less than his life-long friendship with Perne, is enough to repel any such suggestion. But he just could not afford to stay on at Pembroke. Cecil was evidently very ready to be convinced of his suitability for Trinity : he was appointed within a month of his letter.

Nothing could show more clearly than such rapidity of promotion the high estimate of Whitgift both in Cambridge and outside. The University was very restless. Those who were familiar with it—Cecil the Chancellor, Parker the Archbishop, Grindal of London, Cox of Ely—seem to have agreed in discerning in Whitgift the man demanded by the occasion. In him they found the clear-headedness and loyalty, the strength and determination needed to take the lead both against teaching which did not accord with their policy for religion and against conduct which did not conform. If one may be allowed to modernise the Queen's pun on his name, he was their "white-headed boy".

Chapter Two

Protestant Discontents

CAMBRIDGE was restless. The cause was not merely the tension which is apt to arise when old and young are associated in government, though that undoubtedly seems to have been a factor in the troubles. But even more serious was the fact that the University had been infected by the Vestiarian controversy, itself a symptom of much deeper discontent.

When Elizabeth became Queen, she was faced with a situation which might well have depressed the most spirited young woman of twenty-five. The country was at war with both France and Scotland; internally, the Spanish Ambassador remarked that everything was in "hurly-burly and confusion", for there were "neither funds nor soldiers nor heads nor forces". The only hope of survival seemed to lie in the creation of a national unity fired by intense patriotic enthusiasm. From the very first, and increasingly as the years passed, the Queen herself provided the focus for the latter with her deep understanding of her people, her skill not only in choosing but in managing her agents, her almost uncanny flair for the international politics of her day, her gift of saying the right thing at the right time, and even, perhaps, her love of pageantry. But the first requisite was to create unity in a nation divided and confused by the religious upheavals of the last dozen years. Nor was the task made easier by the return from the Continent of those who had taken refuge in protestant centres there while Mary was Queen. They were, in truth, a contentious and difficult body who could not even agree among themselves. At Frankfort their wranglings had been a scandal, and an attempt to unite all by a common programme before they came back failed. Of their conscientiousness there can be no doubt: it compels real respect. But it often expressed itself in a detailed scrupulosity which is one of the main dangers of protestant individualism. Their return did not make the national problems any simpler of solution.

Of the Queen's own religious beliefs and preferences it seems useless to speculate. Few have been more skilful than she in concealing their inner thoughts and motives even from contemporaries. But it was confidently expected that she would make changes; indeed, she could not accept the Roman allegiance of Mary without denying her own legitimacy and claim to the throne. It was in complete assurance of change that the exiles jubilantly returned. But the Queen was not disposed to have her hands forced by unordered enthusiasm. It was strictly enjoined that no changes were to be made until they were authorised, and that, meanwhile, there should be no preaching. When Parliament met in January 1559, Sir Nicholas Bacon, the Keeper, stressed the need for "uniting the people of this realm into an uniform order of religion, to the honour and glory of God, the establishment of His Church, and the tranquillity of the realm". Beyond question that was the royal policy. The Queen wished for such a settlement in religion as would conciliate and unite the greatest possible number of her subjects. The Supremacy Act declared her authority as "Supreme Governor", with power to visit the church and correct all heresies and abuses and to exercise her power through such persons as she nominated to act on her behalf. The Uniformity Act ordered the use in church of the Second Prayer Book of Edward VI with only a few changes. But two of them were significant. In the Communion service the words of administration were so formulated as to suggest real reception by the communicant, thereby eliminating the possibility of the view that the service was only a memorial. Secondly, it was ordered that "such ornaments of the church and of the ministers thereof . . . shall be retained and be in use . . . as were in this Church of England . . . in the second year of King Edward the Sixth". That meant, in effect, the retention of all the catholic vestments in church—cope, alb and chasuble for the celebrant at Communion, the surplice at other services, and the full episcopal habits for bishops. The Second Book of Edward VI had more simply only required for bishops a rochet and for other clergy a surplice at all services. But at Frankfort even the more conservative party had dispensed with this minimal requirement of a surplice for their minister. To the returned exiles the new rubric therefore seemed a step so retrograde as to be incredible. Sandys (afterwards Archbishop of York) wrote to Parker that his "gloss" was "that we shall not be forced to use them, but that others in the meantime shall not take them away, but that they may remain for the Queen"—a strange gloss, surely, on "be in use". That the protestant element in the Commons none the less accepted the act can only be explained by supposing that the Queen insisted on this item and that they knew that if they rejected it the bill would fail and church services would continue legally as they had been under Mary. But they obviously assumed that this was only a first and temporary step.

The Queen's intention was otherwise. To maintain clerical vestments and customary ceremonial, even at a reduced level, was the surest way to advertise the continuity of the church in England against Swiss innovation. It was also the method most likely to conciliate, if that were possible, the large number of her subjects who were still sentimentally attached to the ways to which they had been accustomed, even though they had been alienated under Mary from the Papacy. To have given way about vestments would probably have offended far more than it would have appeased, and would have destroyed all hope of a national church to which all but extremists on either side could give their allegiance. Such wisdom, however, was beyond the reach of the enthusiasts back from Switzerland. They would not be satisfied with anything less than was done in what they called "the best reformed churches"; what had been customary in the Roman church was by that mere fact condemned. Their worst fears about the vestments were confirmed when the Royal Injunctions of 1559 ordered specific outdoor dress for the clergy—"such seemly habits, garments, and such square caps" as were customary in Edward's reign. Not only were the clergy in church to wear the massing garments of the Roman church: even out of doors they were to be marked out as a class distinct from the ordinary Christian, like the priests of former times.

There were, of course, many other things which the returned exiles regarded as objectionable. Pictures in church and windows of stained glass, images, the placing of the holy table where the altar had stood, the use of organs—anything which differed from Genevan simplicity—were condemned. The limitation of the right of preaching to those licensed by the bishop and the provision of Homilies to be read by those who had not such licences seemed to rob the hungry sheep of the food they needed. As time went on the catalogue of faults they found grew in size and detail. But at first the battle was centred on the matter of clerical attire. Nor was objection to it confined to a small body of ignorant and unimportant fanatics. Coverdale, when he took part in the consecration of Parker, wore a cassock but no vestments. Jewel referred to his episcopal robes as "relics of the Amorites", and not only he but all the most eminent of the Elizabethan bishops who had been abroad—Cox, Grindal, Horne, Sandys, Parkhurst, Bentham—"laboured all they could against receiving into the church the papistical habits, and that all ceremonies should be clean laid aside". In the end, as Grindal puts it, they "judged it best . . . not to desert our churches for the sake of a few ceremonies and those not unlawful in themselves." That is a constant theme, though not all agreed that the ceremonies were not really "unlawful". But they feared that if they refused office the field would be open to unsuitable (that is, papistical) ministers. They did not break away, but they did steadily hope for further reforms.

At first the signs seemed promising. The authorities were too busy dealing with Romanists to have time to attend to excesses on the other side. For example, when the visitation of the diocese of London was accompanied by unseemly bonfires of church furniture and ornaments (some of which were in fact legally ordered to be used), no one was punished. But it gradually emerged that the Queen and Archbishop Parker did not mean to make (or allow) any further changes. She refused to allow Parliament to interfere, and he (often at her instigation as Governor) tried more and more to prevent disobedience and unlawful preaching.

With Parker it was not a matter of policy or conciliation but of conviction. His ideal was a "reverent mediocrity", a reformed, not a new, national church which did not make a complete break with the past nor start afresh, as it were, from the beginning. It was to keep catholic orders and traditions, purified from abuses. All that was essential for salvation was to be found in the Bible and nothing contrary to the Bible was to be allowed. But between things plainly commanded and things explicitly forbidden there seemed to be room for things indifferent. In regard to such matters, the local church, he held, was free to make its own rules, naturally having regard to the usage of the early church, but free also to maintain the customs even of the Roman church if they were laudable. Such a national church Parker conceived as an autonomous member of the Church Universal, independent alike of obedience to Rome or imitation of the new continental churches, free both from mediæval superstition and from narrow literal Biblicalism, catholic in its respect for primitive usage. He firmly believed in authoritative rule : "God keep us", he wrote, "from such visitation as Knox have attempted in Scotland : the people to be orderers of things." He could see that the matter of clerical habits was really unessential; but it was important that legal orders should be obeyed. "Does your lordship think that I care either for cap, tippet, surplice or wafer bread or any such? But for the laws so established I esteem them."

Parker was firm, just, kindly. In fact, he was ideally fitted to carry out what seems to have been Elizabeth's policy of broad toleration combined with orderliness. At first he had difficulties with several of his fellow bishops who were anxious to carry reform farther. But little by little, induced partly by his authority, partly by royal pressure and very much by the unreasonable (as it seemed to them) intransigence of the extremists, they gave him firm support.

Apparently it was never possible to enforce the use of full eucharistic vestments. The bishops soon recognised this by allowing a cope and surplice to suffice at the Communion service, and surplices at other times. Later on Parker required the cope only in cathedrals and colleges. But there was no relaxation of insistence on the surplice, which now assumed a sort of symbolic significance between the contestants. Only so can we explain passions it seems to have aroused. There were other things, too, which aggravated discontent. In 1561 the Ecclesiastical Commissioners took steps to prevent the churches from being reduced to Helvetic simplicity. The separation of the chancel from the body of the church was to be firmly marked, the seating in the choir was to be as before, chancels were to be cared for and the holy table decently covered. A royal proclamation forbade the removal of stained-glass windows.

In other words, churches were, as far as possible, to look as of old except for the removal of images and the bringing of the table into the body of the church for the rare Communion services; they were to be kept reverently and cleanly with the holy table as the dominant feature, not the pulpit.

The outcome was an attempt in the Lower House of Convocation in 1563 to effect further reforms—the abolition of Saints' days, of crossing at baptism, of the universal necessity of kneeling at Communion. This move was only defeated by one vote, and that after proxies had been taken into account. Nothing could show more clearly how effectively the ardent reformers were pressing themselves forward as leaders. After their defeat, they seem to have abandoned the hope of realising their aims through Convocation and betook themselves to non-conformity in the most literal sense. They did not separate from the church, but simply disobeyed its rules, hoping by such direct action gradually to effect the changes they wanted. The outcome was confusion. There is a famous paper dated early in 1565 which gives an account of varieties of usage (it is thought to describe churches in London). The prayers were read sometimes in the body of the church, sometimes from the chancel; some kept the order of the Prayer Book, others did not; some wore surplices but not all. In some churches the table was duly kept in the chancel, in others in the body of the church, sometimes but not always properly covered. At the Communion, some celebrants wore surplice and cope, some surplice only, others neither; sometimes a chalice was used, sometimes a common cup; sometimes men kneeled to receive, sometimes they stood, sometimes they sat. The variety of clerical headgear out of doors —square cap, round cap, button cap, hat—was astonishing. The Queen was furious at such goings on. In January 1565 she sent to the Archbishop a letter in which she roundly declared that varieties and novelties, some of which she flatly ascribed to "contention and vain love of singularity", had crept in "for lack of regard . . . by such superior and principal officers as you are". The Archbishop and the other bishops were ordered to see to it, and if any of the bishops would not help, the Archbishop was to report the fact to the Queen, who meant not to suffer such persons to remain in authority. The letter no doubt expressed the Queen's mind, though it was in fact drawn up by Cecil and apparently corrected by Parker. Its violence was really directed against those bishops who were lax towards non-conformity. But it plainly meant that something had to be done.

The most striking result was Parker's *Advertisements* of March 1566, signed by him and five other bishops, of whom three were of the Ecclesiastical Commission. The exact legal authority of the *Advertisements* has been much discussed; but they put beyond question the policy which the Commission and the Archbishop meant to enforce. The only obvious concession was the disappearance of the requirement of a cope at Communion in parish churches. The surplice and the outdoor apparel and all the other points to which the extremists objected were firmly retained, and strong measures were to be taken to stop unsatisfactory preachers.

Chapter Three

Master of Trinity and
Vice-Chancellor

BOTH Oxford and Cambridge were affected by the
Vestiarian trouble, though to different degrees. In
Oxford the Dean of Christ Church, Sampson, and
Humphrey, President of Magdalen and Regius Professor of Divinity, refused to conform. They do not
seem to have had a large following, but their eminence
compelled attention. It was to the Universities that
Parker and the government had to look for educated
preachers if their ideals for the church were to be
effectively put before the nation : blatant non-conformity there could not be ignored. In 1565, therefore,
Sampson and Humphrey were summoned before the
Ecclesiastical Commission. There were long arguments, but they refused to give way at all, even to the
Bishop of London's surely very modest plea that Sampson should "now and then, in the public meetings of
the University, put on the square cap". The argument
was conducted in a seemly and academic way, and
punishment was not savage. Sampson lost his Deanery,
but through Parker's intervention did not suffer long
imprisonment, and was in the end provided for. Humphrey seems for a short time to have withdrawn from
Oxford, but he kept the Presidency of Magdalen and,
later on, at the price of some concessions to conformity,
became Dean successively of Gloucester and of Winchester. There was no vindictiveness in the action
taken against them : it looks more like a demonstration

to show that non-conformity was not going to be winked at.

In Cambridge, all along much more closely identified with the reform movement than Oxford, dislike to the retention of the old ways was not confined to a few learned men, but was violent and widespread, especially among the younger and more excitable residents. In January 1565, for example, the Senate authorised the removal and destruction of painted windows on which the inscriptions seemed to approve prayers for the dead. Later, a sermon in St. Mary's incited to a more general destruction of such windows —and the Heads dared not take action against the preacher. In September, it was decided to remove and sell vestments and ornaments stored in the vestry of Great St. Mary's. No doubt it was their knowledge of the explosive atmosphere in Cambridge which led the Vice-Chancellor and Heads, together with Whitgift (alarmed perhaps by what had been done to Sampson and Humphrey), to write to Cecil in November the letter already mentioned against insistence on the traditional garments. How well grounded were their fears was shown at St. John's where, about the beginning of December, some three hundred of the younger members of the college appeared in chapel without surplices and changes were made in the administration of the Communion. The Master was away at the time (it was said, on purpose), but did not on his return make any attempt to check the innovations. It is alleged that similar irregularities took place at Trinity about the same time, though the evidence is not conclusive. What is certain is that Cecil, the Chancellor, himself a Johnian, took a very serious view of the affair : he reported it to the Queen and, ordered by her, wrote a threatening letter against this "lewd leprosy of libertines" to the Vice-Chancellor, bidding him take firm steps against it. The Master of St. John's was forced to subscribe a paper promising correction of affairs in his college.

The Chancellor's firm action, followed by the publication of Parker's *Advertisements* which, despite much almost riotous opposition in London, were firmly enforced, seems to have put an end to actual disobedience in Cambridge. But it was clear that the younger residents—both undergraduates and Regents—were full of passion for further change. It was, therefore, a wise step to strengthen the Heads by the nomination of Whitgift to the Mastership of Trinity in 1567. He at once, characteristically, required "due observation of the statutes" of the college; even if they were now out of date, he insisted on their being kept until they were formally amended. His position must have required tact as well as strength, for the college numbered among its fellows Thomas Cartwright and (shortly after Whitgift's appointment) Walter Travers, who were to be the real leaders of the presbyterian movement in the English church. For a time there seems to have been no great trouble, though Cartwright was apparently one who consistently refused the "habits" or surplice, and Travers was difficult. Years afterwards, Whitgift said that he had by "due punishment" so wearied him that he left the college for Geneva; otherwise he would have had to expel him for nonconformity.

Meanwhile, Whitgift's favour with the authorities still increased. The Queen made him one of her chaplains. The Bishop of Ely in 1568 appointed him to a prebend in Ely cathedral and to a living near Cambridge. Possibly it was this easing of his financial position combined with increased administrative work which led him to resign the Regius Professorship in 1569, thus unwittingly opening the flood-gates. For he was succeeded as Regius Professor by the holder of the Lady Margaret chair to which, in turn, Cartwright was elected. It was really a turning-point in Whitgift's life, and marked the start of the movement to opposing which his main efforts were thereafter directed almost continuously.

Cartwright was already a leader in Cambridge, as his election to the professorship showed. A few years younger than Whitgift, he was a man of real scholarship whose intense sincerity and strictly ordered life rightly won respect. Bred at St. John's, he had withdrawn from Cambridge rather than conform under Queen Mary. On his return he was made a minor Fellow of Trinity, was recalled to a fellowship at St. John's, and then in 1562 returned to Trinity as a major Fellow—a progress which suggests that his abilities were highly valued. In 1564 he was one of the four who were chosen to conduct a learned disputation in the presence of the Queen. When he preached in the University pulpit, the church was packed. He had all the qualities—learning, eloquence, zeal, austerity—which were calculated to attract the devotion of the younger dissident members of the University. Early in 1570, as Professor, he began to lecture on the Acts, comparing the organization he thought he discerned there with the contemporary ecclesiastical arrangements. Assuming that the New Testament provided a fixed pattern for all time, his teaching was naturally very critical towards the church of his day in England. He suggested that the whole system of government and discipline which had been so carefully preserved from the mediæval church ought in fact to be swept away; that historical continuity should be abandoned for an organization modelled strictly on New Testament lines. He thus gave the first public hint that the Church of England ought to be refashioned entirely.

Here was something quite different from the ordinary criticism of details—clerical attire, the use of unleavened bread and kneeling to receive at Communion, the signing with the cross and the interrogating of sponsors at baptism, the use of the ring in marriage, the veiling of women at churching, the growing use of organs, the altar-wise position of the holy table, licences for pluralities and non-residence. All those were matters which the puritans (regularly so named after 1567) had raised : they could be corrected without fundamental change. But the whole constitution of the church was now called in question—and Cartwright's lectures were crowded.

Complaint was immediately made to the Chancellor, Cecil, by the Vice-Chancellor and others in Cambridge. Even Grindal, now Archbishop of York but still in London, was alarmed. Moved, apparently, by news from Cambridge, he urged Cecil to write to the Vice-Chancellor "to command Cartwright and all his adherents to silence", and to prevent his admission to the degree of D.D. he was about to seek. The Vice-Chancellor vetoed the granting of the degree and there was great commotion. For Cartwright had much support in Cambridge : at least thirty-five residents, not all of them young, signed one or more testimonials in his favour. Cecil was statesmanlike and refused to give orders, but assured the Vice-Chancellor and Heads of his support in any endeavours they should make to maintain peace and order. Later, realising how important the matter was, he charged Cartwright "not to deal any further in these kind of questions" until further order was taken, though he did not think him "of any arrogance or intention to move troubles". But some of the Heads, thus encouraged, inhibited Cartwright from lecturing at all. It is plain, by now, that the real pressure was coming not from the Chancellor of the University but from the Heads in Cambridge. It is also fairly certain that among them Whitgift was the leading spirit. For when Cecil only acquiesced in the silencing of Cartwright, it was he who took upon himself to write that "I think your Honour doth not fully understand Mr. Cartwright's opinions" and to explain what they were.

His letter also reveals that Whitgift had been to see the Chancellor and had advised him of the need for reform in certain of the statutes and ordinances of the University, no doubt provoked thereto by the troubles over Cartwright's D.D. It is striking testimony to the estimate in which Whitgift was held that the Chancellor had at once, apparently, told him to "draw a draught" in consultation with others. Whitgift now says that it is almost ready to be submitted. In the event the new statutes, of which Whitgift was thus the chief promoter and deviser, received the royal seal in September. They were oligarchic rather than democratic. There was a notable change in the balance of power in the University. The Regent Masters lost their dominant position and the Vice-Chancellor and Heads became almost a governing body.

In December, Whitgift himself became Vice-Chancellor. Armed with the authority of the new statutes and supported by other Heads, he took the final step against Cartwright and deprived him of his Lady Margaret lectureship. Every chance was given for recantation: Whitgift was even ready to argue the points raised by Cartwright if the latter would agree to a written rather than a spoken disputation. But Cartwright refused to withdraw. It is only just to him to point out that he does not so far seem to have been looking, as most puritans already did, to continental churches for his model. As yet, indeed, he had not been abroad. His criterion was the New Testament as he understood it : he did not yet positively suggest the full presbyterian form of government. But archbishops and archdeacons should be abolished, with all other officers not mentioned in the New Testament; bishops and deacons should be recalled to their primitive functions of preaching and prayer in the one case and of care for the poor in the other. Government should not be by chancellors and officials, but by the minister and presbyters of the church, and ordination should not be by the sole authority of the bishop but by election by the church. Such supposedly biblical teaching of course made an immediate appeal to young men who had little appreciation of tradition and who looked to the Bible as the only defence against the customs of Rome. ("The only straight way . . . to keep from going astray is the Word of God," said a puritan pamphlet a few years later.) The unpopularity of the bishops for enforcing clerical habits also, no doubt, was in Cartwright's favour. But in Cambridge Whitgift had his way : he deprived him, and now stood out more clearly than ever as the champion of authority and the established order.

Deprived of his chair, Cartwright went abroad and was for some time at Geneva—his first visit there. But he had not lost his fellowship at Trinity and he came back in the early months of 1572. By September Whitgift had once more taken firm action against him and deprived him of his Fellowship also. The ground for this was that Cartwright had failed to observe a college statute which required that he should take priest's orders within seven years of becoming an M.A. At first it looks like an act of petty persecution on Whitgift's part, and he has been accused both of spitefulness and tyranny. In fact, if Cartwright was to lose his Fellowship for that cause, he should have done so about five years previously; and anyhow, the requirement that Fellows of colleges should take orders was very widely neglected without any such dire results. But it seems likely that Cartwright by his turbulence practically forced Whitgift to take such action.

Writing to the archbishop, Whitgift says that Trinity had been as quiet a college as any in Cambridge, but now "clean contrary marvellous troublesome" which he can ascribe "to no cause so much as Mr. Cartwright's presence here". He had only recently discovered the breach of the college statutes, he says (very surprisingly); if he had known and acted on it sooner, he could have saved himself much trouble and the college much contention. He adds that "their whole purpose is to make me weary because they take me to be an enemy to their factiousness and lewd liberty". It is impossible not to wonder whether the axe would have fallen if Cartwright had been a loyal and quiet colleague; but it is also hard not to admit that in a sense he invited his fate. To be sure, it was just the sort of thing his conscience would force on him. It was some time in these years, too—the exact date is not known—that Travers seems to have withdrawn. Anyhow, by 1574, he was on the Continent.

There was, naturally, agitation in 1572 in Cambridge against the new statutes Whitgift had procured for the University, and a petition against them was signed by no fewer than 134 members of the University, including many who afterwards reached high positions in church or University. Richard Bancroft, later Whitgift's right-hand man and his successor as Archbishop of Canterbury, was actually one of the signatories. But they were all young men, and the Chancellor, advised by the two Archbishops, and the Bishops of Ely, London and Bangor, refused to take any action. The objectors, when interviewed, accused Whitgift of trying to "terrify" voters in a scrutiny, so that they dare not vote according to their conscience for fear of displeasure. The Heads denied that there had been any intimidation; but the mere suggestion of its possibility shows what a dominant—even if not dominating —position Whitgift now held.

Despite his victories, however, both in Trinity and in the University at large, Whitgift seems for a time to have thought of leaving Cambridge. Whether he was momentarily wearied by such opposition, or whether he wished for more leisure for his literary work, is not known. But in September several Heads joined in a letter to urge the Chancellor to continue to support and encourage him lest, moved by the contention and trouble in his college and the railing caused thereby, he should leave it, which "the whole body of the University would lament". For he was "wise, learned and wholly bent to the execution of good laws and statutes". The Heads felt that they "could not want him".

Whitgift did not at the moment resign. But in fact his interests and influence were already spreading beyond academic affairs. In 1571 he was appointed to preach at the opening of the Canterbury Convocation. He spoke, characteristically, of the authority of synods, of the enemies of the church, to wit puritans and papists, of the use of vestments and ornaments, and of many things to be reformed in a future synod. Despite his firm dislike of unauthorised changes, he was much too honest and sincere not to admit that there were serious blemishes in the church. Some of them, indeed, this very Convocation attempted to correct. Besides approving the Articles in the form in which we now know them, it approved canons which were directed to providing a better educated and more devout clergy, greater seemliness in the care of churches, stricter oversight of the lives of parishioners. It was even ordered that churchwardens should have the duty of reasoning with adulterers, usurers, drunkards, and of reporting them to the incumbent for sterner measures if they did not amend. In particular, the abuse of excommunication, the almost frivolous use of which for slight offences much angered the puritans, was to be checked. No minor officer but the bishop alone was now to pronounce such sentence; he, too, was alone to authorise the commutation of penance and so prevent the wealthy from avoiding a humbling punishment by having it commuted to a privately paid fine. Pluralities, also, and non-residence were to be limited. Such measures, of course, would not meet all the puritan complaints, but they do show a real willingness on the part of Convocation to recognise and try to meet such criticisms as were fairly directed against the spiritual condition of the church as distinct from its organization.

In the autumn of 1571 Whitgift was made Dean of Lincoln (to which office was added in the following year a prebend in the same cathedral). Parker, in October 1571, gave him a dispensation to hold the Deanery, together with a prebend in Ely, the Mastership of Trinity, the rectory of Teversham and one more benefice (as yet unnamed). However convincing may be the proof they offer of Whitgift's growing recognition, such promotions are a startling commentary on the aspirations of Convocation to check pluralities! The next year, as Dean of Lincoln, he was elected to the important post of Prolocutor (really president) of the Lower House of Convocation. It is pleasant to record that one of his two "presenters" was Humphrey, now Dean of Gloucester, who spoke highly of his merits. It is a tribute to both of them that Whitgift should have won the loyalty of one who had been so sternly dealt with for non-conformity a few years before. As Prolucutor, Whitgift was charged along with his two "presenters" to consult with others and draw up for presentation to the Archbishop a list of matters still requiring reformation. The result was the canons of 1576, published (with slight alterations) by the Queen's authority. As spokesman Whitgift doubtless had much to do with their formation; they show once more a real attempt to nourish the spiritual life of the church by correcting weaknesses and abuses. There is most anxious concern for the educational standards of ordinands and for continued clerical study, while unlearned ministers and preachers are to be excluded. For the laity there are to be regular sermons and teaching of the catechism. Once again, commutation of penance is to be strictly controlled by the bishop, and the ecclesiastical authorities are ordered actually to try (that is, not to overlook as they sometimes did, in the case of powerful offenders) all who are reported to them as guilty of offences. The canons offer real evidence of continued efforts after improvement with which Whitgift was intimately associated.

Chapter Four

Presbyterianism

SUCH mere crumbs as Convocation was prepared to offer entirely failed to satisfy the puritans whose fears had been increased by recent events. The Marian bishops had indeed been deprived, but they had not been put to death; many Marian priests were still allowed to serve parishes, though their loyalty to the Church of England was suspect. Laity who at heart were true to the Roman allegiance were widely left unpunished through the device of occasional attendance at their parish church. Little attempt was made to search them out and punish them and, since about 1567, they had been confirmed in their old obedience by the ministrations of emissaries from abroad. In 1569 there had been an outbreak in the North, which at first had some appearance of success, in favour of the old religion. In 1570 the Papal Bull had been issued which declared Elizabeth excommunicated and deposed, and absolved her subjects from their oath of allegiance. In 1571 there was a plot, engineered by a papal agent, Ridolfi, to murder Elizabeth and set Mary Stuart on the throne, with the Duke of Norfolk as her husband. It was true that the bull largely misfired: it put English Romanists in an impossible position as potential traitors without provoking any foreign power to try to displace Elizabeth. It was true that the Ridolfi plot was easily broken up by Cecil who knew all about it, and that Norfolk was executed. But the Queen firmly refused to allow Mary Stuart to be put to death and equally firmly refused to search the inner thoughts

35

and consciences of her subjects provided they would attend the parish churches as lawfully ordered. The puritans were alarmed : all their hopes seemed to hang by a thread. At any moment the dagger of an enthusiast (who would be sure of the Pope's blessing—his approval of the massacre of St. Bartholemew's Day in 1572 was proof enough of that) might end the Queen's life, and with Mary Stuart on the throne (she was obviously the nearest claimant), supported by Catholics at home and by Spain abroad, a return to Romanism would seem inevitable.

Moreover, apart from such fears, the puritans' own position semed to be worsening. Despite early violent protests, Parker's *Advertisements* were proving effective. Even the bishops who had at first been opposed to clerical vestments were now, impelled by royal authority and, no doubt, irritated by vexatious opposition, firmly set to insist on conformity. A good many of the extremer puritan clergy were deprived in the years after 1566, a certain number resigned, but the great majority seem to have been forced into line. By 1568 Grindal was able to say that the controversy about the habits was dying down. Moreover the increasing episcopal care to control unlicensed or unsuitable preachers meant that the keener puritans had less chance than ever of legitimately venting their complaints in church. It must have seemed the last straw when, in the summer of 1571, all preaching licences dated before May 1 were cancelled (for all the clergy were not permitted to preach, but only those specifically licensed to do so). The Archbishop also began to require from prominent puritan ministers a subscription of acceptance of the Prayer Book, the apparel, and the recently passed Articles of religion, which included the statement that the church had power to decree rites and ceremonies if they were not actually contrary to God's word.

Puritan pressure seems now to have turned to the

House of Commons, where many members were determined supporters of their views. But their efforts there were thwarted by the Queen herself. In 1571 a bill was introduced to effect changes in the Prayer Book which would have removed many of the features to which they objected. Its proposer was promptly sequestered for a short time, and the bill was forthwith dropped. The Queen also refused to approve a bill, passed by both Houses, requiring Communion once a year, an attempt to detect concealed Romanists. She was not prepared to accept such a testing of inner conscience. In 1572 a milder bill to permit the bishops collectively to sanction variations from the Prayer Book was summarily suppressed by a royal message that no bills about religion were to be presented unless previously considered and liked by the clergy—a not very hopeful prospect with the bishops of the Upper House of Convocation in their mood of hostility, and Whitgift the acknowledged spokesman of the Lower House.

The puritans now took a step which was to prove momentous. A small number of them, meeting in London, decided that an address to Parliament should be drawn up. It appeared before the end of June 1572 as *An Admonition to the Parliament*. It was never formally presented : it hardly could be, as both authors and printers were liable to punishment under the censorship regulations. But that mattered little, for it was, in fact, a popular appeal to the general public; actually, the preface is addressed to "the Godly readers". Its success was immediate and resounding. It was clear, direct and seemingly simple, written with force and at times acrimony, but without the personalities and scurrility which spoiled some later puritan pamphlets. Its obvious passion, marred by no trace of self-seeking, was infectious. Above all, its statements were bolstered by copious marginal references to the Bible, an immense asset at a time when the "Geneva" English version, clearly printed and easy to handle, was readily available and greatly cherished by both gentry and middle classes. No wonder that its plain hard-hitting, without any of the tangled arguments customary in theological disputes, had impressive effect.

The *Admonition* marks a clear stage in the development of puritan non-conformity. There is still no desire to break away and form separatist churches, only to reform still further the existing church. Nor are the old complaints about details—surplices and wafer-bread and so on—dropped. They are taken over but almost obscured by passion for re-fashioning the whole government of the church on presbyterian lines. Cartwright had criticized the church order of his day as not biblical. The criticism is now supplemented and completed by the explicit advocacy of presbyterianism in place of episcopacy, with the "best reformed churches" consciously quoted as a model. The "Kingdom" of the "Lordly Lords" must down "because their tyrannous lordship cannot stand with Christ's Kingdom". The whole organization is wrong; ministers were not "according to God's word proved, elected, called or ordained". In the New Testament they were "preachers now bare readers" of the homilies provided for those not licensed to preach. Now they are so ignorant that "like young children they must learn the catechism". They "run fysking from place to place", to try to catch the favour of patrons, and "covetously join living to living". There should be equality of ministers instead of various grades. The writers claim that they have followed the Prayer Book "so far forth as we might", but list twenty-one objections to it, rather on the same lines as before. They are violently critical of dispensations for pluralities and non-residence, of patronage, of ecclesiastical courts, and even of the Ecclesiastical Commissioners appointed by the Queen, who are described as for the most part "papists" : "three of them would be enough to sting a man to death". But, though all the old complaints are repeated, it is clear from constant suggestions that the authors thought the remedy for all ills was to be found in elders to whom, with the ministers, all authority should be transformed. Their office was, according to the New Testament, "to govern the church with the rest of the ministers, to admonish, to correct, and to order all things appertaining to the state of the congregation". They should take the place of "chancellors, archdeacons, officials, commissaries, proctors, doctors, summoners, church wardens". Exact details of organization are not given. But there must be "equality of ministers", and every congregation should have "a lawful and godly seignory". For "to the ministers, seniors and deacons is the whole regiment of the church to be committed".

No summary can do justice to the pithy force and effectiveness of the *Admonition*. It provided a resounding battle-cry. From now onwards a strong body of puritan non-conformist opinion was definitely presbyterian. Moreover, although Sampson had been one of those who planned the *Admonition*, the leaders were mostly new men, younger than those who had protested only against the keeping of traditional ornaments and customs.

The immediate sensation caused by the *Admonition* can be judged by the fact that already, before the end of June, the Bishop of Lincoln attacked it when preaching at St. Paul's Cross. Even he, apparently, admitted the justice of some of the charges it raised : indeed, Convocation was already trying to deal with the scandals of pluralities and non-residence and ignorant clergy. But its main purpose could not be tolerated by the authorities : it would have cut away precisely that historic continuity which both the Queen and Parker so greatly valued, and without which there is little reason to suppose that the bulk of the nation would have been satisfied, despite all the clamour of the puritans. Steps were therefore at once taken. Search was made for the authors and printer of the pamphlet with a view to their punishment, and Whitgift was entrusted with the writing of a reply. The printers could not be found, and in August Parker complained to Cecil (now Lord Burghley) that it had been twice reprinted and with additions; he suspected that the mayor and aldermen of London were "not willing to disclose the matter".

It is true that in July Field and Wilcox, two young London ministers, were arrested and admitted that they were the authors. They were kept in prison till October, when they were tried and condemned to imprisonment for a year. But they were popularly regarded as martyrs and had sympathy and support from influential circles. One did not have to be a presbyterian to see that some of the criticisms of the church of the day were valid. By March, even the Council was pressing the Bishop of London to urge the imprisoned writers to conformity so that they might be treated with more favour! The Bishop found them a sore burden. Though he took them from prison and quartered them in the house of one of his archdeacons, yet in April he complained that all the blame for their imprisonment was laid on him; that he had letters in their favour from noblemen, and that "there is such resort unto them" that they were a real nuisance to their guardian. Later, he describes them as living "in great jollity, having great access to them"; indeed, "the people resort to them as in popery they were wont to run on pilgrimage". He thought—and was probably right—that they would do less harm if set at liberty.

Whitgift obviously regarded his commission to produce an answer as a matter of urgency. Already in September, in his letter to Parker about Cartwright's loss of his Fellowship, he said that he had ended his confutation and that part of it was "written out fair" for criticism. In October he sent to the Archbishop the finished book. He must have worked with great energy and concentration. For the *Admonition*, despite—

perhaps because of—its popular appeal, could not be lightly answered. It demanded careful thought and research. Before the *Answer* was actually published there appeared from a secret press, towards the end of 1572, *A Second Admonition to the Parliament.* Usually, though not with certainty, attributed to Cartwright, it is much less telling than the original *Admonition.* There is even greater bitterness against the bishops and "the pope of Lambeth", but it lacks incisiveness and the power to grip. Moreover, despite its explicit claim that, as the former book told not so much how to reform as what to reform, this is to show "how to do these things", its order is irritatingly confused and its nomenclature baffling. But it does attempt some sort of presbyterian outline for the church.

There are only two sorts of minister, it is maintained, the Pastor and the Teacher. Apostles, prophets, evangelists who, in Ephesians, are named with them are here lightly dismissed as "rare and extraordinary functions". (Even the biblical pattern is not, it seems, sacrosanct.) Oversight of the whole parish and administration of the sacraments belong to the former, exposition of the Scriptures to the latter. With them, in each parish, are to be associated others called governors or assistants or elders, chosen by the parish and admitted to office by the laying on of hands by the minister. Collectively they are to form the "Consistory" which is to administer the affairs of the local church and to apply discipline, though excommunication requires the assent of the whole congregation so as to avoid a tyranny like that of the bishops. Deacons are not a grade in the ministry, but must simply tend the poor and report their needs to the consistory. It is important to observe, however, that the organization is not to be purely congregational. Ministers of neighbouring parishes are to meet in "Conference" for Scripture interpretation, to consider the affairs of the "circuit" and to examine and, if need be, rebuke each other's "demeanour".

Moreover, the appointment of ministers in the parishes is to be made by the conference, not by the local churches alone, though their approval is required. A minister so appointed may neither leave his parish nor be dismissed without the consent of the conference. There is also a suggestion, not elaborated, for the formation of provincial or national synods, including presbyters as well as ministers, for considering "great causes of the church". Despite the many biblical references, it is hard not to feel that the writer's model has really been "the best reformed churches" rather than New Testament practice, especially in the elaborate arrangements for discipline alike of ministers and laity.

Whitgift's *Answer to the Admonition* appeared possibly by November 1572 : at least by February 1573. Inevitably it had less popular appeal than the *Admonition*. For the criticisms there crisply made could not be met by mere brief negations. There had to be careful argument, close examination of Scripture, consideration of history. The main portion of the *Answer* defies analysis, for the *Admonition* was reprinted and answered section by section and sometimes sentence by sentence. But there are certain general considerations at the beginning which are still of great importance. The main scheme of the *Admonition* really rested, apart from its rejection of abuses which were admitted, on certain unproved assumptions. Whitgift begins by very clearly exposing them. First, the newly proposed arrangements are not really so biblical as it was pretended. "The Scripture is most untolerably abused and unlearnedly applied, quoted only in their margent, to delude both such as for lack of learning cannot, and such as either for slothfulness or some prejudicate opinion will not, examine the same." In the body of the work he constantly substantiates this charge, quite successfully. Many of the references given in the *Admonition* do not, in fact, support, and often have really nothing to do with, the assertions in the text. It was a devastating criticism in its suggestion both that the "platform" of the *Admonition* was not really so scriptural as it was claimed to be and that its authors were not quite straightforward.

Next he lays bare the assumption, which is not based in fact either on reason or on biblical warrant, that the New Testament provided a model for all times. It is simply to "ignore the diversity of times" to say that because such and such things were not in the Apostles' times they ought not to be now. To assert that everything is forbidden which is not explicitly commanded in the Scripture is "so far out of the way and so erroneous that it is not tolerable"—a point which he fortifies by pointing to things for which some arrangements had to be made if the church was to function at all and for which none the less there was no biblical direction. He objects also to the view that anything used in the Pope's church was by that mere fact now forbidden. Finally, he suggests that where Scripture is not clear "if either godly councils or ancient fathers were anything at all regarded of these men (as they be not, such is their arrogancy), this controversy might soon be decided".

It is impossible not to admit the force of such arguments which, in fact, seriously lessen the force of the *Admonition*. In their reasonableness and balance and practical sense, as well as in their lack of sectarian narrowness, they are entirely typical of Whitgift, a born practical administrator. So is his general summing up. Nothing is to be regarded as necessary unto salvation save what is contained in or to be gathered from the word of God; equally no ceremonies, discipline or government are to be tolerated which are against the word of God. "But that no ceremony, order, discipline or kind of government may be in the church, except the same be expressed in the word of God, is a great absurdity and breedeth many inconveniences." Such

43

was, and remained, Whitgift's fundamental belief. It is surely reasonable and is certainly Anglican.

At the end a short section is devoted to the *Second Admonition*. Its main thesis is regarded as having been met by the *Answer to the Admonition*. But its plan is described as "a confused platform without any sound warrant of God's word" and (here speaks the administrator) "a fantastical device, tending to the overthrow of learning, religion, yea the whole state and government of the commonwealth". How true were the last words the next century was to show. It should perhaps be added that the *Answer* was not such as would turn away wrath. No more than his contemporaries was Whitgift mealy-mouthed. The puritans were likened to the Pharisees and the Anabaptists, and one passage suggests that they were already showing such traits as later on provoked mockery. "These, walking in the streets, hang down their heads, look austerely, and in company sigh much and seldom or never laugh." They "think it a heinous offence to wear a cap or a surplice; but in slandering or back-biting their brethren . . . in disquieting the church and state, they have no conscience".

With great rapidity, Cartwright's *Reply to the Answer* appeared in April 1573 from the secret press, firmly maintaining the presbyterian platform. It was eagerly received, and soon signatures were being collected to a promise to stand by it to the death. A royal proclamation ordering the surrender of the *Admonition* and all books defending or agreeable to it had little effect. In November the Council issued threatening and scolding letters to the bishops to proceed against non-conformity in their dioceses, even imprisoning the obstinate. And in December the Ecclesiastical Commission took the drastic step of ordering Cartwright's arrest. He avoided it by fleeing the country. Undaunted, and encouraged by the Archbishop, Whitgift set himself to the production of his *Defence of the*

Answer against Cartwright's *Reply*. It appeared in 1574. He knew it was "something big", but he hoped not tedious. In fact, its dimensions are forbidding; in a modern edition it fills two and a half large volumes. But it is important in that it comprises nearly all the literary remains of Whitgift which we have. The method is as in the *Answer*, but is now even more complicated. The argument is rearranged in twenty-three tractates, each reproducing the relevant parts first of the *Admonition*, then of the *Answer*, then of Cartwright's *Reply*, and ending with Whitgift's *Defence*, on each point meeting Cartwright clearly and impressively. Still more than the *Answer* it is incapable of brief analysis. But one or two points stand out. Cartwright, in his *Reply*, had introduced a note of personal bitterness (after all, he had just lost his fellowship at Trinity). Whitgift does not escape the infection—even his earliest and laudatory biographer admits that "the greatest, or rather only, fault in him was choler". Whitgift was conscious of his weakness and apologised that he had been "thereunto greatly provoked".

The predominant impression on the reader is not of the irritation but of the massive learning displayed. Not only are the early fathers quoted with familiarity, but the leading protestants—Calvin, Zwingli, Peter Martyr, Bullinger, Beza—are tellingly cited in refutation of the *Reply*. Moreover, Whitgift is able frequently to show that Cartwright had in fact twisted what was said in the *Answer* and then replied to his own misrepresentation and not to what Whitgift had actually argued. There is a list of fifty-one "untruths and falsified authorities". Most significant of all is the revelation of Whitgift's own very liberal-minded views. What he maintains is that the Anglican arrangements are legitimate, not that they are exclusively so. He does not seek to unchurch other churches, for "there is no one certain kind of government in the church which must of necessity be perpetually observed". Even in the Apostles' time, there were "divers manners of ordaining and electing ministers". Therefore ordaining may rightly belong to bishops, but "I do not say only to bishops". So Rome is recognised as a church, though in error; the protestant churches on the Continent are acknowledged. But equally the episcopal form of the church in England is justifiable. If there are faults in it (which he was much too honest and sincere to deny), care must be taken to attribute them where they belong, not to the system, but to the shortcomings of those who administer it. Such a position may not seem satisfactory to high Anglicans : there is no suggestion that bishops, however desirable, are a necessary part of a true church, still less that apostolical succession is vital. But it was Whitgift's view, and, for his day, extremely tolerant; though Cartwright, too, was scholar enough to agree that ceremonies might differ with circumstances, and that the Church of England was a true church, although he thought presbyterianism more biblical. In defence of his view, Whitgift fought vigorously both against papalism and presbyterianism in the Church of England. That church, over whose fortunes he was to preside for twenty years, owes him a lasting debt of gratitude for his championship.

Abroad, Cartwright continued the debate with a *Second Reply* in two parts. But it had small effect : it was wordy without adding anything essential. Indeed, his original *Reply* soon lost its hold even among his followers, its place being taken by the *Full and Plain Declaration of Ecclesiastical Discipline* of 1574. This was an English translation (probably by Cartwright) of a Latin original written by Travers, his late colleague at Trinity. It was much more suited to the popular taste than either the *Reply* or the *Defence*, less involved and less cumbered with biblical references. It is also a good deal more open to easy criticism, and it is noteworthy that Hooker, trying to meet the full force of the presbyterian position, devoted much more attention to Cartwright than to Travers. In fact, some of the arguments of the *Discipline* could hardly have passed muster had it not been assumed that Cartwright had made out his case. It is, for example, quite boldly stated that Christ must have left a perfect rule, perpetual for all time; if we do not admit that, we "spoil him of his kingly office"—a very high-handed manner of dealing with an issue which depends on evidence. There are other strange things, too. "Doctors" are now introduced as the second order in the ministry, no doubt representing those called "teachers" in the New Testament. Presbyters, flatly against all the biblical evidence, are treated as a subdivision of the deacons—and yet they alone (in one passage) have the right to propose men for the ministry. It is admitted that that was not so in the Acts—but there were special circumstances there! On the other hand, the influence of "the best reformed churches" is increasingly shown both in the elaborate discussion of discipline and the increased power of the presbyters. Actually, though the title of "bishop" is still retained from the New Testament to cover the pastors and doctors, the whole organisation suggested is really presbyterian. There is even a hint of sheer congregationalism in the suggestion that the making (and if need be the removing) of ministers is in the power of the local consistory, although the desirability of co-operation between neighbouring churches is recognised. Despite its vulnerability, the *Discipline* was important. For the next ten years it became the rallying point of the nonconformists. It expressed the form of government which they wished to establish in the Church of England and against which Whitgift had to struggle.

Chapter Five

Last Years at Cambridge

HAD Whitgift chosen to continue the literary contest, there is little doubt that his reply to the *Discipline* would have been vigorous and effective. In fact, for the future, he seems to have preferred to fight presbyterianism administratively. For the time being he remained in Cambridge where there was much for him still to do. When the complaint was made about the new statutes, it was he who advised the Chancellor whom to consult about them, with the result that they were left unchanged. He was again Vice-Chancellor in 1573. But most often he emerged in connection with ecclesiastical matters. He had already been a member of a Royal Commission to enquire into the conduct of a Provost of King's who was suspected of Romanism, and had joined in removing him and, apparently, even in ordering the doing away with the organ in the college chapel. At the end of 1572, he was again prominent, along with the Vice-Chancellor, in burning a collection of ornaments, books and vestments suitable for the Roman services which had been kept concealed by Dr. Caius.

But the main trouble in Cambridge was caused by the puritans. Whitgift's *Answer* was unpopular: a "scandalous libel" against him was secretly set up on the door of the Schools, and he was openly attacked in the public pulpits. Various preachers, including two Fellows of Trinity, his own college, expressed nonconformist or unorthodox views. Such cases fell to the Heads, in the first instance, for discussion, and there is evidence that Whitgift played a leading part among them. When, in 1576, there was trouble at St. John's between some of the Fellows and a puritan Master, one of the charges against the latter was that he had not rebuked a preacher in their chapel who had set himself to confute Whitgift's writings. Evidently to the puritans Whitgift was the arch-enemy. The outcome at St. John's was that Whitgift was one of the commission appointed by the Bishop of Ely to settle the affairs of the college—and the puritan Master was removed. Before Whitgift left Cambridge it seemed as though his battle there had been very largely won, at any rate for the time being. A few months after his departure, the Vice-Chancellor could assure the Privy Council that he knew of none in the University who refused to attend the University Church; a year or two later, a letter asserts that the trouble about cap and surplice is over, and Mr. Cartwright forgotten.

But Whitgift was also a busy member of Convocation, as has been noted, occupied with drawing up the canons of 1576. In 1574 he preached before the Queen a sermon which must have been much to her liking. It was characteristic of the preacher and was so much approved as to be immediately printed. There are no great flights of oratory or feeling after deep mysteries, but rather a closely argued discourse, scholarly in tone but very practical in application. It was really an attack both on the "common people" and on the "preachers". The former, "most unapt persons to deal in such causes" are full of disputes and questionings about religion, of curiosity, and of criticism of their superiors. The preachers, flattered by the compliments of such hearers, are so puffed up that they are "bold to propound anything so that it taste of novelty and please the people, though it tend to the disturbance of the church, the contempt of magistrates, and the breach of good laws and orders". The sermon illustrated the firm and reasonable attitude of the level-headed administrator alike to the foibles of the multitude and the unrestrained claims of enthusiasts. He even had a word of censure for some of the leading men of the day who, for their own purposes, supported the puritan attack on church and bishops; men who, "under the colour of religion, seek confusion and with the shadow of reformation cloak and cover their usury, their ambition, their minds desirous to spoil the church". There were indeed many such, some of them near to the Queen. It was to Whitgift's credit that he had the courage, even in her presence, to denounce them. Naturally, no names were given, but in fact the Queen did herself from time to time support her favourites in their attempt to gain possession of church property. The sermon, no doubt, was less than just to the best of the puritan party, who were men of high ideals and great moral purpose, not mere tub-thumpers. But it was realistic in its insistence that there were in the movement dangers to peace and good order, while the common-sense exposure of the spiritual pride which is based either on ignorance or on flattery was very necessary.

No less prudent was a reply Whitgift gave in 1575 to an enquiry from the Bishop of Ely who sought his views about a scheme for forbidding by law the holding of more than one living and for the restoration to the parochial incumbents of impropriated parish tithes in the hands of bishops and other spiritual men. On the face of it, both pluralism and the alienation of tithe seem to be obviously indefensible. But Whitgift, with the administrator's eye, saw below appearances and advised that such matters were to be "very warily" dealt with. He realised that the points at issue had a financial as well as a spiritual side. Most livings were now so poor that, if pluralities were entirely forbidden, the result would be a "beggarly clergy; which would be the decay of learning, religion and in time of the church also". He even suggested that such may have been the aim of the proposal, so as to make the clergy more than ever dependent on their rich patrons. Besides, he argued, a really good man is probably much more able to see that several livings are properly served than is a bad man to look after even a single one. As to tithe diverted from incumbents to bishops and cathedrals, he pertinently remarked that there was no suggestion in the scheme by which the lay holders of tithe should also give it up. He was very certain they would not. The only sufferers would be "cathedral churches, bishoprics, colleges and other places of learning", the impoverishment of which would be to the serious detriment of the church. The balanced goodsense of such arguments is undeniable. If they seem to lack higher vision, it should be remembered that Whitgift was being asked about a possible act of Parliament; his business at the moment was to estimate practical results, not to preach ideals. It is significant of the estimation in which he was now generally held that such a man as Cox, the Bishop of Ely, old, but able and very experienced, should consult him on these practical matters.

Despite the calls made on him by preaching, controversial writing, Convocation and University administration, he remained a conscientious and devoted Master of his college. His rule no doubt was strict. The Fellows were expected to observe the statutes, the scholars were held to their public disputations and exercises. At a time just after nearly every writer who had spoken of the Universities had lamented their decay, such strict government was of the greatest value. He gave example as well as precept. He was himself constantly to be seen carrying out his duties, regular at prayers "which he never missed, chiefly for devotion, and withal to observe others' absence, always severely punishing such omissions and negligences". Equally, he usually dined and supped in the common hall so as to ensure mannerly behaviour and "by his example to teach them to be contented with a scholar-like college diet". His successor as Master testified to his prudent and peaceful rule and the resulting quiet and moderation. The growing reputation of the college in his day is proved by the eminence of those who were members of it. No fewer than five who were Fellows while he was Master subsequently became bishops, to say nothing of others who attained high office in the church. He had "divers earls and noblemen's sons to his pupils". Just after he became Master, Edward Coke of Norfolk joined the college; Lord Keeper Bacon sent his two sons Nicholas and Francis there; at the end of Whitgift's time, Robert Devereux, later second Earl of Essex, arrived. It cannot be doubted, says the historian of the University, that "his efforts contributed in no small measure to raise" the college "to the proved pre-eminence which it has so long and so brilliantly maintained".

He was, obviously, destined for promotion. As early as 1575 Archbishop Parker had suggested his name, with others, for the bishopric of Norwich, but it was not until 1577 that he was raised to the episcopal bench. On the Queen's nomination, he was elected Bishop of Worcester, confirmed and consecrated in April and finally resigned his Mastership of Trinity and left the University, apparently never to see it again, in June. His farewell sermon in the college chapel is said to have moved his hearers to tears. When he set out for Worcester he was escorted on his way by "a great troop of Heads and others of choice account in the University". His work had been well done, and he had won the real esteem of the University.

Chapter Six

Bishop of Worcester

THE account of Whitgift as Bishop of Worcester given in the *Life* by Sir George Paule is brief, but draws an attractive picture—and Paule was qualified to speak. He joined Whitgift's household almost at the beginning of the Canterbury period, and rose in the end to be Controller of it. He would therefore be admirably placed to gather information. The impression he gives is that of a bishop conscientious, full of activity, friendly, much given to hospitality, exercising great personal influence. Whitgift was liked both by gentry and by the poor, and used his position to promote peace in a turbulent age. On one occasion, for instance, there was like to have been a fray in Worcester between the followers of two knights who were at odds. He gave instructions for them to be brought separately to the palace, well guarded, and there disarmed; meantime he talked to the two contestants and so settled affairs that they were permanently reconciled. He made a point of being on happy terms with the influential men of the city, and was commonly at home at the time of the Sessions and Assizes so that he could entertain justices and judges; his home was a meeting-place where friendly intercourse was easy. In fact, he made himself really pivotal to the civil life of the county. Thus, almost at the end of his time there, the Privy Council referred to him a quarrel between two gentlemen who were disputing about the course of the Avon, and obviously trying to interfere with it, to the great injury of the humbler folk in the district!

Besides acting as the friend of peace and quiet in the diocese, he was assiduous in performing his clerical duties more narrowly conceived. He was a zealous and regular preacher. Unless prevented by affairs of state, he preached every Sunday either in the Cathedral or some parish church, his sermons being the more effective because they were enforced by a "pious life, answerable to his religious sentences". "His gesture and action in the pulpit", says Paule, who must often have heard him, were "grave and decent, his words coming from him so fatherly, and comely . . . without affectation, yet always elegantly . . . full of good and sound learning . . . so singularly applied that he much affected his auditory therewith." He carefully prepared his sermon notes beforehand lest, if he merely trusted to memory, his sermons might become "pratling". He also encouraged others to preach by his mild comments on their shortcomings instead of daunting them by excessive criticism. He was always ready to take up the protection of the poor, whether clergy or laity, against unjust oppression. He was, in fact, a good diocesan bishop as well as a leading figure in the county.

None the less, he had his difficulties. In those days the position of a bishop was not an easy one, and the Elizabethan episcopacy has at times been too harshly judged when this has not been realised. Bishops were expected, on the one hand, to keep up large establishments and to entertain freely. They were hotly attacked if they did not. On the other hand, they were constantly being impoverished—not to say robbed. The law which allowed the Crown during the vacancy of a see to exchange royal for episcopal property resulted in the loss to the bishops of good manors in return for revenues which were not really equivalent. Some sees, indeed, had now become so poor that their occupants could only make both ends meet by holding prebends or rectories as well. Consequently, some of the bishops

strove in a way which now looks unseemly to recover
dilapidations from their predecessors, and some of them
made long leases of episcopal lands on terms very
favourable to the lessees, no doubt in return for a substantial immediate consideration but to the impoverishment of their bishopric for years to come. Those bishops
who were not yet poor were the constant objects of
lay greed, often with the support of the Queen herself
if one of her favourites was involved. The struggle of
the Bishop of Ely to keep his house in London was not
an isolated case by any means; Sandys only just managed to prevent Bishopthorpe being snatched away
from the archiepiscopal see of York. It would be wrong
to suggest that all the bishops were saints, untouched by
the strongly acquisitive spirit of the age. Many of them
were worldly and a few died rich men. But all the time
there was strain, even for the best of them, either to
get or to keep what was their due. Very wisely did Parkhurst write, at the beginning of the reign, "Let others
have their bishopricks; my Cleve (his living) is enough
for me. Many of the bishops would most willingly
change conditions with me; though one or two perhaps, a little ambitious, might decline doing so."

Certainly Whitgift was not ambitious in any usual
sense of the word : he desired only to serve God in the
Church of England. Nor was he worldly—he was a
simple man, unmarried, without a family to provide
for. But at Worcester he did not escape the common
episcopal lot, which indeed his experience well illustrates. To begin with, there was the matter of first-
fruits, the payment to the Crown, not indeed of the
whole of his first year's income as a bishop, but of a
very substantial portion of it. This he was completely
excused, "a princely and extraordinary bounty", says
Paule : it was a real proof of the royal favour. Even so,
he found the income of his bishopric seriously impaired
by long leases of manors and lands made by his predecessors. In particular the rent-corn of his two best

manors had been granted to a Mr. Abington who was cofferer or under-treasurer to the royal household and whose wife was an intimate of the Queen. Whitgift's first attempt at recovery was met by letters of the Queen in support of Abington, though it was doubtful if the lease had ever been legally valid. Whitgift then applied himself to some of his influential friends—the Earl of Leicester, Hatton, Walsingham—and Abington consequently agreed to forgo the corn rents so long as Whitgift was bishop if he could resume them afterwards. That would have meant a long-term loss to his successors and Whitgift refused it. In the end, he paid three hundred pounds out of his own pocket to redeem the leases. But it is doubtful if a bishop less fortunate in high-placed friendships would have succeeded, even at such a price, in recovering alienated church revenues.

Then there was an attempt to deprive him of Hartlebury Castle, his official residence, by the so-called "concealers", men empowered by a royal commission to search out property which had been held in the past for "superstitious uses" and which should, under the law, have therefore now passed to the Crown but had been "concealed". The "concealers", inspired by the knowledge that the more they discovered the richer they would be, were a real menace, confusing and bullying the clergy. One list of their interrogatories looks veritably like an episcopal visitation : it is small wonder that simple and ignorant ministers dreaded their attentions. So outrageous was their conduct that the Queen had frequently to cancel their commissions. Even Whitgift did not feel himself safe. When they came to his parts they did not deliver their commission to him (to whom in fact it was addressed) but to the sheriff, thus plainly showing at whom they were really aiming. Alarmed, Whitgift at once wrote to Burghley for his protection. In the end he did not need it : the "concealers" failed to convince the jury of their

claim. But his fears are an index of the dangers
threatening even episcopal property.

His efforts on behalf of his clergy were as strenuous
as for himself. He is reputed to have made a strong
appeal to the Queen on their behalf for protection
against "concealers", warning her, plainly, of the
dangers of sacrilege, but so tempering his words that
despite his "affectionate plainness" he still "continued
in her favour". On another occasion he interfered
against an attempt to disturb his clergy by a bogus enquiry into the legality of their presentations. He was
constant, too, in his attempts to improve the quality of
sermons in his diocese. When he arrived, he found that
the presentation to all the prebends in the Cathedral
was in the Queen's hands, which seriously checked his
efforts to provide good preachers. By another singular
exercise of royal favour, he managed to secure the
power to nominate to all the prebends so long as he
was bishop.

Then, as he wrote to Burghley, there were two kinds
of men which were delighted in molesting and
troubling him, namely, the contentious protestant and
the stubborn papist. His diocese does not seem to have
been as much troubled as were some, but he had to exercise constant vigilance. Even before he left Cambridge he had orders from the Queen, who disliked
puritans, to insist on conformity and especially to put
an end to "prophesying". On the other hand, the
Council, which feared papists, was insistent in its pressure on him, as on other bishops, to enforce measures
against recusants. Thus, actually prior to the Act of
1581 about church attendance, he was required to
furnish a list of those who did not go to their parish
churches. His first report was apparently not regarded
as detailed enough, and the Council returned to the
charge with elaborate instructions on procedure, including a schedule of names of those whom he should
call to assist his enquiries. All who had previously been

reported, and others whom he suspected, were to be examined with great exactness; for the counties in his diocese other than Worcestershire the Council suggested the names of gentry whom he might employ in similar investigations since he could not conveniently do it all in person. Similarly, before the formal proclamation to recall English youth from study in foreign seminaries, he was commanded to summon the parents or friends of such (whose names were again given in a schedule) and exact bonds of them "in good sums of money" for the return of the young men—and his archdeacons were to find out if there were other parents to be similarly dealt with whose names were not on the schedule. The next year, after the passing of the act for Retaining the Queen's Subjects in their Due Obedience, the Council turned to him to enforce it in his diocese by diligent search and enquiry, trying to persuade obstinate refusers but reporting to the *Custos Rotulorum* and Justices of the Peace those who would not obey, so that they might be dealt with as the law directed. Ten months later there was another order from the Council to the same effect.

It might reasonably be supposed that with the Queen's explicit instruction to deal strongly with protestant non-conformists and the Council's repeated pressure on him to enforce laws and proclamations against recusants, added to his regular preaching, the normal administration of the diocese and the part he deliberately took in the affairs of the county, Whitgift's time would be adequately employed. But further burdens were added which show how greatly the government was already coming to rely on him. Shortly after he became bishop he was made Vice-President of the Marches of Wales. The President, Sir Henry Sidney, was at the time in Ireland as Lord Lieutenant, but did not resign his Presidency—pluralism was not confined to churchmen. Doubtless Whitgift did not have the prestige and splendour which was enjoyed by the

President in person, but his was none the less a very important and responsible post involving unceasing care. In the absence of Sidney he really became the chief government agent for the day to day administration of a very wide area covering Wales and the neighbouring counties. There was a constant flow of instructions from the Privy Council to him and the Council of the Marches dealing with an astonishing variety of matters. Some were trivial enough, but perhaps none the less tiresome for that—to see that the fees due to a royal messenger were paid, or to send up to London for trial by the Privy Council a man whose written answers had not been satisfactory.

There were also things of greater moment—to make a certificate for the general musters, to forward evidence concerning some felons whose arrest the Privy Council had ordered, to enquire into a suspected case of murder in Hereford or of High Treason in Wales, or to deal with disorders in Monmouth. There was evidently a good deal of trouble about some rioters who had thrown down "frames" erected by Sir John Throckmorton in Worcestershire, presumably to enclose what was regarded as common land. At times he must have had to walk with delicacy, as when complaints made to the Privy Council about the conduct of some of the powerful Earl of Leicester's agents in Wales were referred back to him and the Council of Wales for action; or when he had to deal with Lord Stafford who had not shown himself sufficiently submissive to the Privy Council. There were, too, constant troubles with recusants, some of high birth, whom the local J.P.s could not deal with. On one occasion he had to report that the wife of Sir John Throckmorton had been attending Mass at the house of a Mr. Edwards and that his son was under instruction from a priest— and Sir John was a prominent man in Worcestershire who had been chief justice of Chester under Mary and for a time Vice-President of the Marches. The Privy

Council inhibited the local justices from dealing with Edwards and his friends and ordered Whitgift to do it, sending him also a list of persons to be apprehended and examined by "such as your Lordship hath already used". Tact as well as firmness would be needed in such cases : a false step might have serious consequences.

In all such manifold affairs Whitgift would have the help of servants and agents, but in the end the responsibility was his; he had, for example, to clear himself to the Privy Council of a charge of having allowed murders and misdemeanours in Worcestershire—a charge which would have been futile if he were not held responsible in such matters. Nor was his position made the more easy by the President. Sidney has the reputation of having been a kindly and merciful administrator, but he was jealous for his authority. When Whitgift was made his Vice-President he was warned by Burghley that he should be careful to inform Sidney of all that he did. Before long, sure enough, Sidney was complaining that he was not properly posted, and Whitgift had to defend himself by asserting that he really had certified him of all that had been done, adding that Sidney had sundry times tried to interfere "at other men's suits" and his wishes had been refused because they were "grounded upon wrong information". Evidently Whitgift's position was not easy. But he seems to have won the complete confidence of the Privy Council, who sent him a letter of thanks when Sidney returned to take up his duties. Indeed, on one occasion when new Justices of the Peace were to be nominated, the Council named one for Worcestershire, together with "such other as the Bishop shall think meet"; for Warwickshire, the Bishop was to name them all. In a responsible and difficult position he had manifestly acquitted himself well.

Sidney returned in 1580, and Whitgift's labours, though he was still a member of the Council, were correspondingly lightened. But he was much worried by

Sidney's suggestion that fines for non-attendance at church should be paid to the Council of Wales. Whitgift felt that if that were done the Exchequer would be impoverished to that extent, and that the money was not really needed by the Welsh Council. He wrote to Burghley to say so.

For the rest of his time at Worcester such extra-diocesan work as was put upon him was ecclesiastical rather than civil. In 1581 he was called into consultation over important matters. There was in the House of Commons a very active puritan element anxious for further steps in reform. The tact of certain Privy Councillors, who were not unsympathetic to puritanism but who were sufficiently near the Queen to know how strongly she resented interference from Parliament in ecclesiastical matters, prevented the House from actually putting forward bills. Certain proposals, however, were drawn up for discussion with the bishops. They were submitted to the Queen, who summoned the Archbishop of York (not, be it noted, Canterbury, who was in disfavour) and told him to answer the proposals in consultation if he wished with other bishops. Whitgift was one of the five whom Sandys called into consultation. He was still very much a junior among the bishops, but it was a wise choice. Though the proposals put forward look harmless enough to the unwary, even in parts desirable, they in fact contained the seeds of a possible presbyterian growth within the church, and Whitgift knew all about that.

The bishops' powers, it was suggested, should be severely checked. No one was to be ordained except to fill a living actually vacant, nor was any to be admitted to a living before the bishop had given notice, invited objections within twenty days and—surely a rather humiliating condition—actually given formal notice that all this had been done and that he had heard the objectors. With a little ingenuity that could have been manipulated to become, in effect, the "calling" of the minister by the parish where he was to serve. Then the bishop was to be required not only himself to be satisfied of the character of ordinands but to assure the Dean and Chapter of his cathedral that he had actually received the testimonials legally required—and even then might only proceed to ordain if the Dean and Chapter, or six learned preachers then present, allowed the ordinand as a man meet and sufficient; which all looked like presbyterian control of the bishop. The canons agreed by the Convocation in 1576 (suggested by Whitgift and the Lower House) and issued with royal authority, had limited the right of commutation of penance to the bishop, for its abuse by minor officials had caused much criticism. Now it was proposed that even the bishop should need the assent of the Dean and Chapter, or six preachers of the diocese, in commuting. The canons of 1571 had sought to limit pluralities to the holding of two benefices at most, within reasonable distance of each other, and had discouraged non-residence. It was now proposed still further to limit, by more exact and cramping regulations, the discretion of the Faculty Court to issue dispensations. Oddly enough, though such dispensations were to be reduced in general, Fellows of colleges who were under statutory obligation to take orders were to be allowed to retain their fellowships even if they did not do so, if they were known to profess divinity—the exact issue on which Whitgift had caused Cartwright to be deprived of his fellowship at Trinity! Had the suggestions been accepted, there is little doubt that they would have seriously upset the balance of power in the church and tilted it in favour of presbyterian instead of episcopal control.

The answer made by the bishops is firm and realistic, showing that practically the proposals would hamper the work of the church, reduce the status and education of the ministry and upset the traditional machinery. The arguments are logical and impressive.

Whether Strype is right in supposing that they were actually drawn up by Whitgift is uncertain. But there can be little doubt that they express his views—indeed, parts look very like what he had already written to the Bishop of Ely—and that he had a leading part in formulating them. The result was the failure of the attempt to insinuate presbyterian movements in the episcopal machine. The Queen approved only such very small changes as the bishops had allowed, and ordered the bishops themselves to effect them by their own authority and without legislation. Once more the presbyterian aims of the zealots in the Commons were defeated; and, once more, Whitgift had taken a leading part in opposing them.

In January 1583 there was further work for him. Grindal issued in his own name, but by order of the Lords of the Council, a commission to him and others to visit the city and diocese of Lichfield and Coventry; the main work fell on Whitgift. Affairs in the diocese were very unhappy. The newly appointed bishop (Overton), presumably in real financial straits, provoked trouble all round by his efforts to collect money. He had driven the citizens of Lichfield to take legal measures against him by his attempt to recover for the see certain "mills, markets, fairs, fish-pools" which they claimed had been given to them by a previous bishop. He had asked the clergy for a special subsidy (for which, seemingly, there was some precedent in that diocese) to help him with his initial expenses. The Dean and Chapter had refused to pay their share. Legal actions followed, each party complaining bitterly that it was persecuted by the other and appealing to Burghley and the Privy Council. This was the real occasion of the issue of the commission to Whitgift and the visitors. It is all very sordid, but it does throw light on the lamentable state of the church—the poverty of bishops, the devices to which they had to resort, their strained relations both with the inferior clergy and the laity.

The next month there was also referred to him as visitor a quarrel which shows the sort of difficulties bishops had to face from their own legal officers. Overton had first of all appointed as his Chancellor a man named Beacon : he had then added to him as joint holder of the post one Babington, who was his own son-in-law. He now was trying, by methods which may have been strictly legal but which could certainly be made to look shady, to get rid of the former completely in favour of the latter. The post was lucrative : one of the documents makes it clear that payment had been made for it, and Beacon proceeded to take action against the bishop in almost every conceivable court, ending with an appeal to the Privy Council. The matter nowadays looks unsavoury; the bishop's action suggests nepotism and was certainly open to criticism, especially when he, who had appointed Beacon, explains that he would now be rid of him because he was unskilful in the law and so unable to give a right judgment, and could not be trusted because he was the bishop's enemy ! Such a man, surely, should never have been appointed Chancellor; and anyhow, if he had really been proved to be such, the bishop should have been free to get rid of him. But the post had been bought as a piece of property. The whole incident shows how little control the bishops really had over their nominally subordinate legal officers; this was especially the case when it came to regulating the fees they should be allowed to exact. The bishops could not, in fact, always control them : they had bought their offices and expected the returns long customary. That was why it proved so hard to reform the ecclesiastical courts.

Whitgift dealt with the troubles quickly and well. In June he wrote to suggest that his visitation should cease and the bishop's authority be restored. (It had been suspended during the visitation.) He explained that Beacon and Babington were now agreed and so were even Beacon and the bishop—though he does not say on what terms; he added that Babington was not really sufficient for the post in question! Presumably, too, Bishop and Chapter were now brought to peace, or Whitgift would not have wished to be relieved. Certainly in August the Chapter agreed to the establishment of a lectureship in the Cathedral to be financed partly by contributions from the prebendaries. The Privy Council (of all people) had first suggested this even before the visitation, but it seems as though it was not successfully established without some prompting by Whitgift as visitor.

About the same time Whitgift was also employed, with others, in drawing up new statutes for the Cathedral in Hereford. It is typical of his methodical care that when they were sent to Walsingham for submission to the Council and approval, Whitgift wrote a personal letter to Burghley to secure his support. Nothing was left to chance. This Chapter also wished to provide for a lecturer in the cathedral and to that end petitioned that they might be allowed to surrender to the Queen a rectory and the chapels attached thereto, which they possessed, in order that she might confirm it to them again "for ever" for the endowment of the lecture. The procedure looks cumbrous. Probably the Chapter feared that if they did themselves what they wanted, the attention of "concealers" might be drawn to the rectory. If so, their fears were justified. For in June Whitgift wrote to Burghley, of whom he says "there is none with whom we of the church either are or may be so bold" for his support against such attempts. In the result, no doubt through this intervention, the lectureship was duly founded. As at the beginning of his episcopate, so to the end Whitgift showed himself a strong defender of the interests of the church not merely where he was directly responsible but wherever he thought he could help.

Chapter Seven

Recusancy and Puritanism

THE six years during which Whitgift was Bishop of Worcester were a period of serious trial, possibly of real danger, for the Church of England. The Settlement was threatened by both papalists and puritans, and the suspension of Archbishop Grindal by the Queen sapped the powers of the church just when it most needed to be strong.

The hopes and courage of the Romanists were rising. The massacre of St. Bartholomew's Day in 1572, and Alva's successes in the Low Countries, naturally suggested that the cause of protestantism was waning on the Continent, and that soon an attack from abroad might be expected. In July 1580 the Queen found it advisable to issue a proclamation against traitors abroad who suggested that an invasion would shortly take place, assuring her people of her confidence in divine support and that the country was fully prepared. Furthermore, the attitude of the Romanists at home was stiffening. The setting up of an English college at Douai (afterwards moved to Rheims) and of a daughter college at Rome for the training of Englishmen for the catholic priesthood resulted, in the seventies, in a stream of well-trained, enthusiastic and fearless seminarists. They, and the Jesuits, were much better equipped than the remnants of the Marian clergy to carry on the fight and to strengthen the resolve of those who still clung to the old religion. Despite the dangers of such mission work in England, the colleges drew a steady stream of recruits from England, young men, often of high ideals, shocked by the condition of the church at home and, perhaps, alienated by the sort of services the puritans favoured. Moreover, the Jesuits, the cleverest of the new evangelists, condemned outright (and with papal backing) the device of occasional attendance at the parish church by which so far many Romanists had avoided the penalties of the law. Recusancy now became almost as widespread and obvious in the south as it had long been in Lancashire and the north.

The government could not remain passive. In 1577 Cuthbert Mayne, a seminary priest from overseas, was arrested, condemned for treason and, after every attempt to turn him had failed, executed in November; though professing obedience and loyalty to the Queen, he would not deny that he would feel himself bound, if called upon, to aid invaders who sought to restore the papal obedience in the country. He was the first, but not the last, to suffer so. Before the end of the reign the list grew to over six score clergy and half as many laymen. Moreover, though the government tried to be gentle—it preferred recantation to what could be represented as martyrdom—nevertheless as the situation grew more tense, torture was applied to prisoners to exact information as well as change of mind. It was so in the case of Campion, the most attractive of all the missionaries, able, learned, saintly. His treatment and his execution in 1581 deeply troubled many, and not only those who sided with him. But it was always maintained firmly by the authorities that he and his like suffered not for their religious faith but as traitors to the Queen. In view of the bull of deposition it is impossible to deny that they might well be legally such —especially, later on, when the Pope declared that the oath of allegiance might be taken and then, at his bidding, broken without sin.

Repressive measures were repeated. The Queen's proclamation of 1580 was followed by others—in

January 1581 recalling English students from catholic seminaries abroad, bidding relatives to report their names and to cease contributing to their maintenance if they did not return, and ordering the imprisonment of all Jesuits and seminarists who were detected. The next year another proclamation insisted that the death of Campion was for treason, since the whole aim of the Jesuit mission was to incite to rebellion. All such agents were declared traitors, and any who harboured them guilty of high treason. Once more all English students in the seminaries were ordered home. In 1581 parliament also took a hand. An act "to Retain the Queen's Majesty's Subjects in their Due Obedience" was passed, asserting that any who claimed to free her subjects from their oath of obedience to the Queen were guilty of high treason; any who aided them were likewise guilty of misprision of treason. The penalty for saying mass was fixed at 200 marks; for hearing it, 100 marks and imprisonment. Any over the age of sixteen who failed to attend their parish church were liable to a fine of £20 a month (no small sum in those days) and to imprisonment if the fine was not paid within three months, over and above any penalty which might be imposed by the ecclesiastical courts. Most striking of all, perhaps, was the energy and vigilance of the Privy Council in the chase of recusants, especially in districts where the local magistrates could not be trusted to see that the laws were enforced. Nothing could more fully reveal the efficiency of the government machine than their "Acts", in which vigour was directed by remarkably accurate information of what was going on all over the country. In 1578, for example, the Bishop of Norwich was warned to look out for a particular priest whose name was known and given. In the autumn of that year the Council actually went to the eastern counties to deal with recusancy on the spot. In Norwich, although three of the recusants were induced to conformity, two had to be put in gaol, and nine others were fined and forbidden to leave the city. In Suffolk, two were imprisoned and four more subjected to house confinement, and the magistrates were warned about papists in disguise. There were similar dealings in Essex; one recusant was entrusted to the keeping of the Treasurer of Walden, to be subjected to the persuasions of two preachers and gaoled if he were not converted! In 1580 the Council was able, typically, to send to the Bishop of Chester a long list of families who had sons abroad for training. He was ordered to exact bonds for their return. In the same year, the Council even had to issue an order to all members of the Queen's household to insist on the conformity of their subordinates, and to dismiss and report to the Council such as would not submit. In Lancashire, the steward of many of the crown lands of the Duchy of Lancaster was a recusant.

The result was a constant stream of suspected persons sent to London for examination and, if need be, torture. Special places, such as Wisbech Castle, had to be set aside to provide room for the imprisonment of the numerous recalcitrants. The Ecclesiastical Commissioners were warned to look out sharply for recusant schoolmasters. Nothing could illustrate the strength and danger of recusancy more strongly than such activity of the Council—unless it be the fact that even such activity was not able to crush it at once. The fines for non-attendance at church often were not paid, and the local magistrates refused to allow distraint to obtain the money. Evidence of trouble comes not only from the north and the eastern counties, but from Shropshire, from Oxfordshire and the neighbouring counties, from Sussex and Exeter. In London, mass said in the Portuguese and Spanish Embassies was attended by Englishmen. Indeed, there was great commotion when the Recorder of London broke into the former and arrested and imprisoned such English as he found there. His zeal appears to have been thought excessive by the Queen and he was punished : she, at least, did not wish to offend a foreign power. But mass was also said in private houses, and the Recorder, a few years later, declared that his court had been "every day occupied with seminary priests, Mass-mongers, libellers and such like"—though once more the Queen interfered sometimes to prevent the full punishment laid down by law. It is recorded that, in 1581, mass was actually said in the Fleet prison.

On the other hand, the puritan movement was still very much alive, though in a less conspicuous way. It had undoubtedly suffered a check at the end of 1573, when the bishops were ordered by the Council, instigated by the Queen, to take strong action against irregularities. In London several non-conformists were imprisoned in December. The most distinguished and ablest of their preachers, Edward Dering, a lecturer at St. Paul's, having been first forbidden by the Council to lecture and then restored by the Council without consultation with the bishops, was finally silenced by express command of the Queen in the same month. Others were arrested the next year—though once more the Council seems to have been more lenient than the bishops : they ordered two to be set at liberty with a mere warning to conform for the future. Still, there was a real effort to control extreme partisans. Five ministers were dispossessed in Northamptonshire, and so on. Moreover, Cartwright and Travers were now abroad and, very important, the printer of Cartwright's *Reply* had been detected and dealt with, as well as several other printers who had been concerned with producing unlawful books.

Thus, in July 1574, Bishop Cox of Ely could write that "Our puritan brethren are now lying in concealment, partly terrified by the authority of our Queen, and partly silenced by a most able treatise written by a most learned man"—a reference to the *Defence* of Whitgift whom he elsewhere describes as "the most vehement enemy of the schismatics, and the chief instrument against them in our church". Even so, Cox knew too much about the puritans to be quite happy: for he adds, "We know not what monstrosities they are hatching in secret". His fears were justified. The puritan enthusiasm and dislike of episcopacy which could not safely express itself in pulpit and the press found an outlet in the so-called "Prophesyings" which were not only permitted but actually encouraged in many dioceses. In theory, the prophesyings were meetings of local clergy for biblical study and conference, and for mutual counsel and correction. The earliest notice of them is at Norwich in 1564, where they were strictly confined to the educated clergy—only those who knew Latin might take part and no one engaged in secular work might even attend. But later these bounds were extended. In 1571, there was the Northampton Model, a serious attempt to stimulate the spiritual life of the local church by the instruction and discipline of both clergy and laity by services and meetings additional to what was required by the Book of Common Prayer. The local ministers met for two hours every Saturday and handled some passage of Scripture "openly among the people", speaking (and no doubt disputing) in turn. The proceedings had the approval of the Bishop of Peterborough.

Strype says such prophesyings were a little later used "throughout most of the dioceses", with episcopal approval, and though such generalisations are to be treated with caution, there is positive proof that such meetings were widespread. The Bishop of Lincoln, thinking them "good and godly, and greatly making to the furtherance of true doctrine", laid down rules for their conduct in Hertfordshire, with moderators appointed by himself and a warning that no stranger should be allowed to speak; the Bishop of Norwich similarly gave orders for "the godly exercise of expounding the scriptures by way of prophesy" at

Bury St. Edmunds. In both cases, the clergy were actually ordered to attend. Obviously the bishops thought that this was at least one way of correcting the clerical ignorance of which there were such loud complaints, and there is evidence that the educated laity approved of such exercises. But they were not without their dangers. They provided an opportunity, despite the Bishop of Lincoln's prohibition, for "falling into controversies of our present time or state", particularly when, as in the Norwich diocese, the bishop allowed some of the dispossessed non-conforming ministers to take part in them lest their hortatory powers should be wasted by the church! The Queen, at least, saw the possibility of trouble. In 1574 at her bidding Parker wrote to the Bishop of Norwich to say that the Queen had willed him to suppress such vain prophesyings. Parkhurst, the bishop, was obviously astonished, particularly as he shortly afterwards had a letter from the Bishop of London and three members of the Privy Council, urging him to allow the exercises to continue provided that there was no heretical or schismatical doctrine. He consulted the Bishop of Rochester, who in his reply frankly approved the prophesyings, provided that they avoided current controversies. But Parker insisted, and the Bishop of Norwich gave way. The whole incident is illuminating. It shows how widespread was the approval of the prophesyings (if they were properly controlled). For the three Privy Councillors who wrote to express approval were Knollys the Treasurer of the Royal Household, Thomas Smith one of the Secretaries of State, and Walter Mildmay Chancellor of the Exchequer, an influential layman. Moreover, in view of their letter, it would seem that this attack on the prophesyings came from the Queen herself and not from the Council; and that it was directed for the moment only against Norwich, for neither the Bishop of London nor the Bishop of Rochester had received similar instructions.

Now, as later, one gets the impression that the Privy Council were, on the whole, not unfriendly to the puritans, that the real drive against them came from the Queen herself.

When Parker died in 1575 and was succeeded as Archbishop by Grindal, the position became very difficult. Parker, like the Queen, had always disapproved of the puritans and their doings; Grindal, as Bishop of London, had been lenient to them, to the great discontent of Parker. This was not due to any laxity, but to high ideals. When he became Archbishop he showed his zeal for improvement, not only by publishing the reforming Canons of 1576 (for which, as previously indicated, Whitgift as Prolocutor of the Lower House must have been largely responsible), but also by an attempt to check the abuses of the Court of Faculties which issued the dispensations for pluralities, non-residence and the like. He was eager to provide a learned, resident, preaching ministry. It was in keeping with his desire for the religious education of the country that, so far from abolishing the prophesyings, he sought to encourage them, though laying down very strict regulations for their inoffensive conduct. They were only to be at places appointed by the bishop and under moderators approved by him. No laymen were to be allowed to speak, nor any dispossessed minister. Any attack on any public or private person, or on the "laws, rites, policies and discipline of the Church of England" was to be instantly silenced. So he sought to direct and control puritan zeal to the support of the established order.

But the Queen had other views. She seems to have wanted simple obedience in the church rather than reasoned conviction reached through argument and exposition. In December 1576, she told Grindal that she thought it good for the church to have few

preachers—three or four for a county—and that otherwise the reading of the official Homilies was sufficient;
and she asked him to suppress completely the prophesyings. In a long letter notable, and almost unparalleled
in that age, save from puritans, for its outspoken
courage, the Archbishop refused. With great wealth of
biblical quotations (some of them indeed not obviously
apposite) he stressed the importance of sermons and
the inadequacy of the Homilies as a complete substi-
tute. The prophesyings he defended as instituted by
the bishops on the basis of Scripture; he quoted by
name nine bishops who had in writing testified to their
value in improving the learning and skill of the clergy,
and declared that he could not "with a safe conscience,
and without the offence of the Majesty of God, give
my consent to the suppressing of the said exercises".
He added a petition that the Queen in dealing with
religious matters should consult with bishops and
divines as in legal affairs she consulted the judges; and
that in all pronouncements she would not deal "too
resolutely and peremptorily". "Remember, Madam,
that you are a mortal creature."

Such language was not likely to conciliate the
Queen, nor to turn her from her purpose. In the event
she simply went over the head of Grindal and issued
her instructions direct to the bishops for the suppression of the exercises, at first by individual letters (Whitgift, even before he left Cambridge for Worcester, had
one) then by general letter to all bishops in May 1577,
threatening to "make some example in reforming of
you according to your deserts" if they did not take the
necessary steps.

Despite the lack of tact in Grindal's approach, it is
at first difficult not to sympathize with him : it does
look as though the prophesyings, if properly regulated,
might have been really valuable. But it is possible that,
in fact, the Queen was wiser than he; they may have
already got so far out of hand that very strong mea-

sures were needed if they were to be prevented from bringing disorder and weakness into the church whose unity was, politically, vital to the strength of the country. It is significant that the Bishop of Peterborough, two years after he approved the Northampton Model, was writing plaintively to Burghley for help against the puritans. The Bishop of Durham thought Grindal wrong to oppose the Queen's measures. So did Cox of Ely, who thought that the exercises should be completely stopped for the moment, to be revived presently with good rules for their regulation. That indeed seems to have been what ultimately took place, for in 1584 there were regulations issued for their conduct by the Bishop of Chester, who claimed that he had the authority of the Privy Council for issuing them and that they had just told him to increase the number of places and occasions for them. The implication is that they were already taking place. Even as early as 1581 Sandys, apparently with the royal approval, set forth a form for their conduct in the Northern Province where the real danger was Romanism not puritanism. It is thus likely that they were never effectively suppressed. For a few years, certainly, by the Queen's command, the bishops in the south could not approve them. Probably they went on surreptitiously and, lacking official oversight, were less controlled than otherwise they might have been and so served to keep alive puritan enthusiasm. On the other hand, they were much less widespread and dangerous than if they had not been checked.

The clash between Queen and Archbishop had serious consequences. In 1577 Grindal was sequestered and confined to his house for six months—"an extraordinary thing", as Strype remarks. Though he was allowed to continue his spiritual functions such as consecration, his administrative work, visitation, institution and so on, was carried on by two lay officials appointed by him on the order of the Council. Sometimes he was himself allowed to act under orders from the Council. At the end of the six months, despite the strong advice of Burghley, he refused to retract or to apologise—and remained sequestered. In January 1579 there was some thought of deposing him, but this was not done, and he remained sequestered, though now two men nominated by the Queen in place of the two he had chosen carried on the administrative part of his work, save when he himself acted under orders from the Council. In 1580, for example, he was ordered to take steps against ministers who preached only, and would not administer the sacraments—and at once did what he could. Such was the position till he died in 1583, though in fact a little time before his death he had agreed to the Queen's suggestion that he should resign. The arrangements for this were not completed before they were made unnecessary by his death.

It was a disastrous episode, as was plainly recognised both by the Queen in agreeing to his resignation as a way out, and by Convocation in a long petition to the Queen in 1580 for his restoration. Just when the church needed not secular control but strong spiritual leadership against both Romanists and non-conformists, its authority was largely undermined and weakened. It would probably be wrong to attribute to this weakness the first serious emergence of clear-cut separatism about this time. Still in fact it was in 1580 that Robert Browne began to collect, along with Robert Harrison, a band of followers in Norwich which formed a separate church based on a formal covenant. He also visited Bury St. Edmunds and encouraged there the puritan element which, with the keen approval of local gentry, was trying to organise itself on presbyterian lines, nominating its own clergy and using a Genevan form of worship. The bishop's representatives were very roughly handled by the local J.P.s. Both the bishop and the justices wrote, significantly, to Burghley for support, not to the Archbishop. In the end Browne was driven to the Low Countries with Harrison and some of his followers. In pamphlets he bitterly attacked those who, though opposed to episcopacy, did not simply break away and form their own churches. This was the real beginning of the separatist movement—though oddly enough Browne himself submitted in 1591 and subsequently held office in the church for forty years. In Bury, however, there continued to be trouble, and two puritans were there put to death. Indeed, there was so much disquiet that the Bishop of Norwich petitioned to be moved to a quieter diocese! It would no doubt be unfair to attribute such troubles entirely to the unfortunate position of Grindal. Sooner or later, separatism was bound to emerge : it was the logical outcome of non-conformity if it could not gain its own way in the church. There had already been isolated cases of it elsewhere : in 1578 the Council had to deal with it in Gloucestershire. But hitherto its supporters had been poor and ignorant. It is difficult not to suppose that the almost fanatical support of the gentry in and near Bury was not at least in part due to the clouds under which the church was labouring.

Chapter Eight

Archbishop of Canterbury:
the Fight for Reform

GRINDAL died on July 6, 1583. On August 14 the Queen nominated Whitgift to succeed him: his election was confirmed on September 23, and he was enthroned on October 23. Such unusual rapidity of procedure—Ely, after the death of Cox in 1581, was allowed to remain without a bishop for over seventeen years—shows both the Queen's determination to put an end to the practical paralysis of the see of Canterbury, and her unhesitating choice of the man to fill it. In fact, when the possibility of retirement for Grindal was under consideration, he himself wished Whitgift to succeed him, and the latter is said to have begged the Queen's pardon for refusing to accept so long as Grindal was alive. But the succession was not in doubt. Nor could the Queen have chosen any man more fitted both by character and inclination to forward the policy she favoured. He was as firmly convinced as Parker had been of the legitimacy of the episcopal form of government and was determined to maintain it. His dealings with Cartwright and Travers had made him fully aware of the dangers threatening from the puritans, the extent of which was not always clearly realised even by some of Elizabeth's chief advisers. Above all, though possessed of real patience and even, at times, kindliness in dealing with opponents, he was a strong man. How much he would have achieved against the enemies of the Church of England had he stood alone it is not easy to guess. But the Queen, having chosen her man, gave him almost unwavering support, and the combination was effective; almost all open puritan opposition had died down by the end of the reign.

As at Worcester, he had at first to face financial troubles. The see was over-valued for first fruits, and some of its possessions had been wrongfully withheld from it. That was the sort of trouble with which he was well qualified to deal successfully. A much more difficult task was to restore the archiepiscopal prestige and authority so seriously compromised in Grindal's days. The Council had formed the habit of issuing instructions, even on ecclesiastical matters, which the Archbishop had simply carried out. At best that was, from Whitgift's point of view, quite intolerable. Ecclesiastical order was for the bishops to administer, not the Council. What made it worse was the fact that several powerful members of the Council were friendly towards the puritans, while some definitely shared their views. Leicester, long known to be their patron, was, till his death in 1588, a strong influence. Sir Francis Knollys, first cousin to the Queen and Treasurer of her Household, was profoundly suspicious of episcopal claims. He had been abroad under Mary, and was only prepared, it seems, to tolerate bishops as the Queen's agents, not as holding inherent authority. Walsingham, principal Secretary of State, was at heart a puritan, and so was his brother-in-law, Sir Walter Mildmay, Chancellor of the Exchequer. Even Burghley, though in public he gave the Archbishop his support and never encouraged law-breaking, was yet not unfriendly to the puritans, and showed himself most anxious that they should not be unjustly or unduly pressed; the number of their appeals to him for help shows that they were not unaware of this. Indeed, for a time he even employed Travers as domestic chaplain, and tutor to his son Robert. The Clerk to the Council,

Robert Beale, expressed himself so violently in a book and so insolently in personal contacts that the Archbishop had to complain of him to Burghley. On the other hand, at first Whitgift was not even made a member of the Council : he did not become so till February 1586—and then only while Leicester was absent in the Low Countries, and to his sharp anger when he heard of it. It was the first time the Queen had appointed a bishop to the Council, which shows how much she already valued Whitgift.

Moreover, apart from personal preferences, the Council was at the moment much more preoccupied with danger from Rome than from Geneva. At home recusancy was rapidly spreading; abroad, Philip was at the height of his power; things were going well for him in the Netherlands and he was known to be plotting an invasion. The puritans, at least, were unmistakably anti-Roman; at such a time, it naturally seemed perverse to check their fervid protestantism by insistence on rules and regulations they did not like and by silencing them in the pulpits. Besides, some of their complaints were obviously justified—there really were far too many unlearned and unworthy ministers, there was too much pluralism and non-residence, the conduct of the ecclesiastical courts was far from satisfactory.

Whitgift, himself far too fair-minded not to recognise such blemishes, vigorously set himself to correct them. He was not deaf to legitimate puritan complaints. If at times he seemed, as he did, to be more concerned to deal with protestant than with Roman non-conformity, it was probably because he knew that the Council could be trusted to do all that was possible to check the latter. Though certainly no friend to the Romanists, it was for him rather to attend to the danger from the other wing which was growing serious. Even in this policy he was at one with the Queen. In the very year before the Armada she is recorded to

have told the Archbishop of York, with her almost uncanny flair for judging a situation, that the puritans
were greater enemies to her than the papists. There are
times when it is impossible not to wonder whether she
did not, in her antagonism, really over-step the proper
limits of visitatorial power, as when she sequestered
Grindal or threatened the bishops (as she did) with
deprivation. None the less, it seems at least possible
that her determined support of Whitgift and her tight
hold on Parliament were what really prevented the
church from being re-modelled in presbyterian form
before the end of the century.

Whitgift acted at once. On October 19, before his
enthronement, he issued to the bishops articles drawn
up in consultation with them, and fortified by the
"most gracious consent and allowance" of the Queen.
They were of uncompromising simplicity and direct-
ness, aimed alike at Romanists and puritans and at the
correction of admitted faults in the church. First of
all, the laws against recusants were to be enforced—
and his covering letter to the bishops instructed exactly
how this was to be done. Minister and churchwardens
were to observe who for the space of a month did not
attend service, once a quarter their names were to be
reported to the bishop or his nominee to be sent on
to the justices and, if they did not act, through "slackness", or if juries would not convict, the bishop was to
pronounce the offenders excommunicate and, after
forty days, liable to a writ to be taken out against them.
Next, all private and family meetings for "preaching,
reading, catechising and other such exercises" were
completely forbidden if attended by outsiders. In
church, none were to preach, read or catechize unless
at least four times a year they said service and
ministered the sacrament according to the Book of
Common Prayer. All preachers and all in orders were
to wear the apparel laid down by the *Advertisements*
of Parker, nor were any to preach or interpret the

Scriptures unless either a priest or a deacon admitted according to the laws of the realm. Nor—and this proved the real bone of contention—was any to preach, read or exercise any ecclesiastical function unless he subscribed before the Ordinary of his diocese or his representative to three statements—one affirming the Queen's supremacy, one asserting that the Prayer Book and Ordinal contained "nothing contrary to the word of God" with a promise to use it and none other, the third allowing the Articles as "agreeable to the word of God". It was the requirement of this threefold subscription, and especially the second clause of it, which roused the puritans to anger and shrill complaint. If these Orders of Whitgift could have been enforced effactually, it would have been the death-blow to nonconformity, its preachers excluded from the pulpit except on conditions they would not accept, its private conventicles forbidden. There followed articles aimed at correcting acknowledged shortcomings in the church. No one was to be ordained except to some definite cure or living (save those in Cambridge and Oxford) nor without due evidence of character and of at least a modicum of learning. Bishops who ordained against this rule were to lose right of ordaining for two years. They were protected, too, against legal proceedings by patrons if they refused to institute unsuitable men presented for benefices. Penance was only to be commuted "in rare respects and upon great occasions", and then only with the bishop's approval and after open admission of fault. Marriage by licence was regulated so as to try to avoid abuse.

Whitgift was not satisfied merely to have the articles circulated to the bishops : he asked also for a return from each diocese of all ecclesiastical persons, their promotions, their degrees and their "conformity . . . to the laws and orders any ways established by her Majesty" that he might be "the better furnished to govern" his province. If there were any hopes that easy-going tolerance of variety was to be continued, they can hardly have survived his sermon at St. Paul's on the anniversary of the Queen's Accession (November 17). It was an elaborate discourse, fortified by innumerable references to the Bible and the Fathers as well as to secular history, concerning the virtue of and the necessity for obedience, both to the bishops and the magistrates, with a cutting reference to "wayward and conceited fellows" who would obey only "what they list, whom they list and wherein they list themselves".

Before the year was out, his power of enforcing obedience was strengthened by the establishment of a new Commission for Ecclesiastical Causes, with himself at its head. Even without this, his power was extensive. As Metropolitan he had the right to visit the whole of his province, which he at once started to do by means of commissioners; he had also the over-sight of such sees as were vacant. None the less, his effective power was immeasurably increased by the setting up of the Commission. It could act in a diocese where the bishop was not zealous: it could pursue the disobedient, if need be, from diocese to diocese, as a bishop could not; it was authorised to punish by fine or imprisonment as well as by mere ecclesiastical censure, often despised; it could summon a suspect without any formal accusation or witness; it could search out unlawful books and their authors.

His policy clear, his equipment fully furnished, Whitgift proceeded to govern. It was not long before there was trouble. Certain ministers of Kent and the diocese of Rochester refused to subscribe as required by his articles. Of their objections some were fundamental, some seem now almost trivial. They didn't like Saints' days, and thought the Litany too long, nor did they approve the reading of the Apocrypha. They condemned the clerical attire. More serious, they thought that bishops, priests and deacons were contrary to God's word, and wanted elders in every church. Some of them condemned the ministering of sacraments in private houses—even the communion of the sick, as well as the private baptism of infants—and wished the people in each church to have the right to choose their own minister. Some frankly asked for the full presbyterian platform of doctor, pastor, senior, deacon. Pronounced contumacious for their refusal to subscribe before the Archbishop's agents, they were summoned to answer at law in the middle of February. Thereupon, in a body, they went to see the Archbishop in person. He showed astonishing patience. Though they seemed to him unlearned and young and such as he would not have ordained, and though their reasons varied from childish and frivolous to irreligious, he spent the whole of one afternoon and the greater part of the next two days in talking to them together or severally. In the end, they still refused to subscribe, and were suspended. They at once appealed to the Privy Council. About the same time, some of the "gentlemen and justices of the peace" in Suffolk wrote to the Council to complain that "painful pastors and ministers of the word" were "marshalled with the worst malefactors" for "matters, as we presume, of very slender moment", though they were in fact breaches of the Prayer Book ordered by law. Nothing could show more clearly how low the prestige of the arch-bishopric had sunk under Grindal than such appeals to the Council over the head of the Metropolitan—unless it was the reaction of the Council itself. They wrote to the Judges of Assize in Suffolk to beware of malicious accusations, and to deal gently with those who "making some conscience in these ceremonies, do yet diligently and soundly preach true religion and obedience to her Majesty". The faults regarded as venial by the Council include refusal to wear the surplice, leaving out parts of the service, and private prayer meetings. The Kentish complaints they referred to Whitgift with a request that he would appear before them on the following Sunday!

This attempt of the Council to control the new as it had controlled the late Archbishop was at once countered by Whitgift. He had in December accepted some of its suggestions for enquiry in the dioceses and forwarded them to the bishops because he approved of them—questions about unworthy ministers, pluralists, abuse of excommunication, excessive fees. But to be summoned, as it were, to justify his conduct to the Council was too much. In a dignified but quite uncompromising letter he asked to be excused. He explained the pains he had already taken with the Kentishmen, and his estimate of the complaints. He was sure they were presumptuous—their visit to him uninvited proved it—and any encouragement from the Council would only make them worse. Anyhow, the refusers of subscription were only a small minority in Canterbury, and in other dioceses, save Norwich. Most preachers had subscribed. He added, pointedly, that he could not be persuaded that the Council really meant to call his doings in question when his authority had been committed to him immediately from the Queen, who alone had the power to judge his use of it. To such a firm rejoinder the Council had no answer. Though some of them resented it (notably Beale, the Clerk), the Council now knew the sort of man with whom it had to deal.

The Kentish ministers remained suspended. Later, in May, when certain of the gentry petitioned Whitgift that they might be restored because they did, in fact (it was said), use the Prayer Book and conform, he remained adamant. He was fully informed about them, and was able to show that they did not, in fact, use the book fully and without alteration, but only as they chose. Anyhow, if they did use the book, they ought to be willing to subscribe to it. No church in Christendom would tolerate ministers who did not obey its rules and rites (a shrewd thrust at those who favoured the Geneva pattern with its severe dragooning). To remove all grounds of complaint, he was most careful to see that vacant places were filled by subscribing ministers. On the other hand, when some ministers were suspended in Sussex, Whitgift himself saw, reasoned with and convinced them, and their suspension was removed. His firmness was plainly equalled by his great patience.

In May 1584, undaunted, he drew up articles and questions to be administered by the Ecclesiastical Commission. The form of process before the Commission cannot fail to appear today both tyrannical and unjust. The examinee, summoned by the Commission, was required to take an oath to answer questions put to him without knowing what they were to be—the so-called *ex officio* oath. The result might well be that, without any witnesses against him, he would, if truthful, be driven to condemn himself by his answers. For years the procedure caused much serious disquiet, and not only among those who suffered through it. But it was a weapon Whitgift refused to forgo. It was a legacy from the mediæval church, where its original object was to enable an accused person to clear himself by oath exacted by his superior : it was thus pastoral rather than judicial in origin. That character it had now largely lost. It was, however, undoubtedly legal, and had in fact been used in the case of suspected papists, and in the Star Chamber and other courts. What made it now so formidable was the searching character of the questions laid down by Whitgift to be put by the Commission to those who took the oath. Had they been ordained according to the legally recognised Ordinal, and did they acknowledge it to be not "repugnant to the word of God"? Had they taken the oath of canonical obedience? Had they used the Prayer Book services, without alteration, and none other, and did they accept it as a "virtuous book, agreeable or at least not repugnant to the word of God"? Had they worn the surplice in conducting services in church? Or refused private baptism to a weakly child, or omitted the signing with the cross or the questions to God-parents at public baptism? Had they varied the lessons, or the litany, or omitted the use of the ring in marriage? Particularly, had they made any alteration, omission, or transposition in the Communion service? Had they taught or written against the Prayer Book, or attended conventicles for the support of such adverse views? Or preached without being licensed by the bishop? And had they subscribed the three articles as required? The meshes of the net were so small that no convinced puritan could possibly hope to escape.

This new move undoubtedly caused a very difficult time for Whitgift; but he never seems to have wavered, or even to have failed in patience. Not only were the puritans, or some of them, evasive, but they secured strong lay support. Whitgift was unmoved by the powerful position of their friends. Not even to Burghley would he give way—and yet the friendship between them and their mutual respect were unimpaired. A well-known puritan in Essex was suspended by the Bishop of London for non-subscription. Burghley (really misled) appealed for him to Whitgift, who firmly replied that the man was in fact a ring-leader and that the Commission would have to proceed against him. When the Council wrote on behalf of men in the Ely diocese, he wrote to Burghley that he had interviewed some of them and was not pressing them, but that they would (if they did not retract) have to be dealt with one by one, at convenient leisure. None the less, he was plainly feeling the strain of it all. He frankly admitted how much gratitude he owed the Lord Treasurer for protection at Court against his enemies, and ended that he was at the point to "say with David *in manibus tuis Domine, sortes meae.* They cannot do more against me than He will suffer them.

And if there be no other remedy, I am content to be sacrificed in so good a cause : which I will never betray, nor give over, God, her Majesty, the laws, my own conscience and duty, being with me." Shortly afterwards (no doubt in self-defence) he sent Burghley a schedule of subscribing and non-subscribing ministers in eleven dioceses : 786 had subscribed and only 49 refused—an impressive result, though it did not, perhaps significantly, include London or Norwich or Peterborough, which were the most disaffected dioceses.

That was in June 1584 : matters came to a head in July. Burghley, continually worried by puritan complaints, had been moved to take up the case of two Cambridge curates who had refused to subscribe. In considering their cause, he had obtained a copy of the questions to be put by the Commission, and he was shocked. He found them to be "in Romish style", "so full of branches and circumstances as I think the Inquisitors of Spain use not so many questions to comprehend and to trap their preys. . . . This is not the charitable instruction that I thought was intended." He had advised the two men not to answer, though he had warned them that if they were disturbers of the church they must be corrected. Whitgift's reply was full and very careful : to retain the support of Burghley, privately, was a very different matter from presenting himself at call before the Privy Council. He maintained that the proceedings of the Commission were legal (which Burghley had admitted), but added that action was never taken against men merely for non-subscription but only for actual breaches of the forms of service prescribed by law, and after conference had failed to persuade. As for the two men in question, they were not what Burghley had been led to suppose, but had really been disorderly, and one of them actually complained of for it by some of the parishioners. If Burghley supported them, he would undo all Whitgift's efforts. Obviously Burghley had been misinformed—but he still did not like the *ex officio* oath. So a few days later there was another letter from Whitgift, stressing his eagerness to satisfy Burghley in all things and to have his approval, but still refusing to abandon the course his conscience dictated. He enclosed two papers, one justifying the procedure by the *ex officio* oath, and the other showing the "inconveniences" of dropping it. Even so, Burghley does not seem to have been happy about it—but the friendship of the two men remained unimpaired. Whitgift could still feel sure that "variety in judgment concerning some circumstances" could not "diminish that good affection in his Lordship, or in himself, which had been by so long time and experience confirmed". And, in fact, despite his qualms and his liking for some of the puritans, Burghley in public supported Whitgift and the laws.

Still the Archbishop's troubles were not ended. In September the Council once more took a hand on behalf of ministers in Essex. But their approach was almost amusingly different from their earlier efforts for the Kentish ministers. There is no idea now of summoning Whitgift to answer for his conduct. On the contrary, the suggestion is that the blame rests chiefly with "inferior officers, chancellors, commissaries, archdeacons and the like", and that Whitgift and the Bishop of London had not sufficiently checked them. Complaints from Essex had forced the Council to look into the "lamentable state" of that county, and they found many "zealous and learned preachers" suspended and many livings vacant, while pluralists, non-residents and ignorant and unseemly ministers were unmolested. They even enclosed lists of both types of minister, and urged tolerance of "diligent, learned and zealous" pastors, though "in some points ceremonial they might seem doubtful, only in conscience and not of wilfulness". But Whitgift was equal to the occasion.

Essex was under the Bishop of London, of whom he said he would make further enquiries. But the Bishop had assured him that none, or very few, of those now said to be unworthy had been complained of or detected as such by their churchwardens at the archdeacon's visitation; and when those who now accused them were asked to send their complaints for investigation by the Commission, they had rather turned to the Council, "hoping thereby to alter the court"—a very significant move. Those suspended, on the other hand, were "chief authors of disquietness" and without further conformity on their part their suspension must remain. Clearly the Council, like Burghley, had been led by their sympathies to act on evidence which was not reliable.

It seems to have been about now, after a year in office, that Whitgift sought the Queen's approval of his policy. He saw her and then sent to her in writing a statement about the condition of affairs. The greatest number, the oldest, wisest and most learned had, he assured her, conformed. The others were few, young in years and of unsettled mind—no doubt an *ex parte* statement. He was on surer ground when he maintained that he had been acting only for the "maintenance of the laws and orders established by public authority", and wondered what would be the outcome if it should be lawful for "common persons and private men, in a settled state, to pick quarrels" and "to innovate what they list, when they list, and so often as they list". We do not know the Queen's answer, but there can be little doubt of her reaction to such arguments. Whitgift's position and authority were now firmly established as against the Council, and were strengthened by the Queen's approval and support.

Chapter Nine

Parliamentary and Other Agitations

WHITGIFT'S troubles were, however, by no means at an end, despite the Queen's support. In the Parliament which met in November 1584 the Commons included a number of forceful and outspoken puritans, who were not to be silenced by the memory of the Queen's displeasure in the past when attempts had been made to interfere in ecclesiastical affairs. In truth they were more excited than ever. Recusancy was spreading; the murder of William of Orange in July had shown the lengths to which the enemies of protestantism would go, and Throgmorton's plot of the previous year, with foreign backing, had shown that even Elizabeth's life was not safe. Actually during the time of this Parliament another such plot was discovered. Parry, a member of the Commons, and one of the Queen's Household, was proved beyond doubt to have been plotting her death, emboldened thereto by a papal dispensation. And yet the Queen seemed to be strangely reluctant to act with energy against the papists. She had intervened when Parry (his treachery yet unknown) was imprisoned in December by the Commons for a too violent speech against a bill concerning Jesuits, and she had procured his forgiveness. Moreover, imprisoned papists were argued with rather than punished—Lancelot Andrewes was sent to those at Wisbech Castle; and when persuasion failed, they were simply allowed to remain as they were.

Besides, now that Whitgift was pressing conformity and subscription, suspicion of the whole Anglican policy was increased. Though it might be true, as Whitgift told Burghley, that the *ex officio* oath was only being offered to those who were really known to be offenders, and that men were not being deprived merely for refusal to subscribe his three articles, the fact remained that a good many of the leading puritans were punished in 1583–4. Wilcox and Field, the authors of the *Admonition to the Parliament,* were respectively deprived and forbidden to preach. When Giles Wigginton, the aggressive vicar of Sedbergh, came to London to preach, he was sent for by Whitgift, offered the *ex officio* oath and imprisoned when he refused it, later to be released only with a severe warning not to try again to preach in the southern province. Aylmer, Bishop of London, earned the bitter hostility of the puritans by his activity, and well-known leaders both in London and Essex were suspended or deprived, though some of them enjoyed the patronage of distinguished friends such as Lord Rich or even Lady Bacon.

It does not seem to have occurred to the puritans that it was not reasonable to expect that church officials should be allowed to hold their posts unmolested while they flagrantly attacked or broke the rules of the church—though, by a strange irony, it was about this time that they disciplined Wilcox himself by the withholding of his maintenance until he came to heel. That, no doubt, was quite a different matter! For what the bishops and the Commission were doing seemed to them to be crypto-Roman. Amazingly, even Whitgift was accused of being favourable to and approved by papists. To the fervid puritan fancy all was of a piece; the officials—bishops, archdeacons, chancellors—were Roman; the clerical dress was Roman;

the Prayer Book, "raked out of the filthy puddle of the popish liturgy", was Roman too.

No wonder that puritan members of the Commons were, so to speak, on edge. Further, their fears and prejudices were constantly fanned from outside. Though exact dates are not easy to fix, there is evidence of a constant succession of petitions and supplications to the Queen, to the Council, to Parliament, to Convocation; from Norfolk, Essex, Lincoln, Oxford, some in verse, some in prose; against Whitgift's articles, against subscription, against the oath *ex officio*, against the Archbishop's power. The title of one such paper frankly reveals the substance of many—"The unlawful practice of Prelates against godly ministers". There is evidence, too, that the puritans in many places agreed to send delegates to London during parliament time to bring pressure to bear on those members who favoured their views.

In such conditions, it was necessary for Whitgift to be very much on guard. The first bill considered and read by the Commons showed their mood : it was for "the better and more reverent observing of the Sabbath"—a matter which was now much exercising the puritans. Great trouble was taken over it. The first draft was superseded by a second, which was the subject of amendments by the Lords and long negotiations between the two Houses before an agreed form was reached, only to be "dashed" by the Queen, so that its contents are not now known. But both the purpose of the bill and the care taken over it were significant. Then there was a bill, also much revised and recast in committee, that parsonages impropriate should be converted to charitable and pious uses which did not, seemingly, pass the Lords; perhaps not unnaturally— no doubt many of them enjoyed the fruit of such impropriations. Then on December 14 there was an unmistakable puritan outbreak. Three petitions were presented to the Commons which would have reversed all

Whitgift's measures—for the liberty of godly preachers, for them to exercise and continue their ministries, and for the speedy supply of able and sufficient ministers in places destitute. The petitions were read but no immediate action taken. Emboldened by this, a Dr. Turner asked that the House should now read a bill and book offered by him heretofore—the book he described as "digested and framed by certain godly and learned men which did tend to no other end . . . than the glory of God".

The book was, almost certainly, practically the book which the English exiles in Geneva in the time of Mary had devised for themselves on the basis of Calvin's prayer book; no doubt the bill was to bring in a ministry agreeable to it. It was a direct attempt to oust the Book of Common Prayer. Even Knollys, for all his suspicion of episcopacy, took alarm. He and Sir Christopher Hatton, the royal Vice-chamberlain (an unwavering supporter of Whitgift), persuaded the Commons not to have them read, assuring them that the Queen would take all measures justly required. The House then turned to the safer subject of a bill for securing the Queen's safety. But two days later they returned to the matter of the petitions, and were persuaded by Sir Walter Mildmay (himself a puritan) to the cautious procedure of reducing them to heads and articles which could be imparted to the Lords, who should then be asked to join the Commons in pursuing the course which should be thought most advisable. At first the Lords were reluctant to interfere, but when they were assured that complaints were coming in from all over the country, they agreed to help, but thought it wise, in view of the Queen's well-known attitude, that such lords as were of the Privy Council should ascertain "her Majesty's pleasure" before further action was taken.

Parliament was adjourned from December 21 to February 6, but the sixteen heads into which the petitions were resolved were communicated to Whitgift. The suggestions made went a good deal farther than those he had helped Sandys to answer in 1581. Ordinands now were to be approved, not merely by Dean and Chapter, but by six resident incumbents; there was still also to be allowed time for parochial objections to be lodged before any incumbent was instituted in a benefice. It was now further proposed that all ministers who did not come up to the standard of learning laid down in 1562 should be suspended and deprived of their livings. Even more revolutionary was the claim that no oath or subscription should be required save what was "expressly prescribed" by the statutes of the realm; that ministers who were diligent and of "good conversation" should not henceforward be troubled for "ommissions or changes of some portions or rite" in the Prayer Book (a wide phrase which would have covered any vagaries); that the archbishops and bishops should try all ecclesiastical cases in person, not through officials; that ministers suspended for refusal to subscribe Whitgift's articles should be restored; that the *ex officio* oath should be abolished; that "exercises and conferences" should be started in every archdeaconry; that excommunication should only be used for major offences, not for mere contumacy, and then only by the bishops themselves, not by their chancellors or officials; that all licences for pluralities and non-residence should be abolished—or at least that the curates engaged by non-residents should be allowed to preach and instruct and catechize in the parish.

No one was more anxious than Whitgift, or strove harder, to obtain an educated and otherwise satisfactory ministry. But if the petitions were granted, practically all that the puritans stood for would be obtained; bishops, it is true, would in name have been left, but with their authority whittled away—powers of ordination checked by local clergy, of filling livings by local option, of jurisdiction by the abolition of their normal agents. On the other hand, non-conforming clergy would be restored, free from any oath, and allowed to use as little of the Prayer Book as they wished, unchecked by the Ecclesiastical Commission. Whitgift reacted at once. He wrote to Burghley protesting against the proposals and tactfully reminding him that "her Majesty loved not to hear of innovations". He also sent to the Queen herself proposals agreed by him and others, though not as yet drawn up in formal manner, for strengthening precautions against unworthy ordinations or presentations, for the restraint of commutation of penance, for the close control of marriage without banns, of excommunication and of pluralities. As these proposals, when duly formularised, were confirmed by the Queen in 1585 at the end of the session, he presumably received her approval of them.

Thus armed, he was ready to meet, along with Burghley and Sandys, the representatives of the Commons when they presented themselves in February to discuss the petitions with the Lords. The Commons received a severe shock. Knollys, reporting back to them, said he must consult the rest of the committee before he could give an account of the answers, for the Archbishop had raised so many points that he could not retail them at once. A few days later, a full account was given. Even Burghley had not been helpful. He had said that the Lords thought many of the suggestions were unnecessary, that others were already provided for, and that the Prayer Book was established by Parliament. Whitgift gave a reasoned and detailed reply, of which we have the account he sent to Burghley. What is most striking is not so much that he made no concessions to the puritans as the congency of his arguments. To deprive unsatisfactory ministers wholesale, as suggested, might raise doubts as to the validity of their past actions, leave too many parishes vacant, and send many men with their families begging; some of the petitions would tend to such liberty and freedom for ministers "as no subject in this land did enjoy"; others tended to "popular elections, long ago abrogated in the church"; others to a cramping of the bishops' effective action. The report of it all, given by their representatives, clearly caused a flutter in the Commons—"divers motions and long speeches"—and they agreed that those learned in the law should consult and resolve on further action.

That was the end of the petitions as such; but the Commons still busied themselves about religious affairs and had to be watched. They were busy with a Sabbath bill and about the return to religious or charitable uses of impropriated livings as well as with the bill about Jesuits and for the Queen's safety. In March they were bolder—there was a bill to allow marriages at all seasons of the year, another for reformation of certain disorders in ministers, another against excessive fees and taxation in ecclesiastical courts. About the last three Whitgift complained to the Queen on March 24: "Albeit, according to your Majesty's good liking, we have set down order for the admitting of meet men in the ministry hereafter" (no doubt a reference to the articles formally confirmed by the Queen a week later), "they passed a bill in that House yesterday touching that matter." It appears actually to have contained a proviso that ordinands should be approved by twelve laymen now. The other two suggestions would interfere with long-established custom.

Before these last bills could be fully passed, Parliament was dissolved, but not without a royal rebuke. In her speech, the Queen admitted that there were "faults and negligences" in the church, "all which if you my Lords of the clergy do not amend, I mean to depose you". But she added that there were "many over-bold with God Almighty, making too many subtle scannings of His blessed will. . . . The presumption is so great as

I may not suffer it . . . nor tolerate new-fangleness"
It was "dangerous to a Kingly rule, to have every man
according to his own censure to make a doom of the
validity and privity of his Prince's Government". She
disallowed the Sabbath bill, the others were not ready,
and the only acts confirmed as the result of all the discussions were one for the Queen's safety and one
against Jesuits and seminarists, ordering them to leave
the country within forty days and to be guilty of High
Treason if they returned, though provision was made
for them to submit by oath to the royal supremacy if
they wished—though those who did so were not for ten
years to come within ten miles of the Queen's person!

Thus none of the specifically puritan points was
achieved, but so far as complaints were directed against
such real "faults and negligences" as the Queen admitted, Whitgift and the bishops were ready to meet
them—so long as it was through Convocation and not
by act of Parliament. Indeed, what we know of Whitgift suggests that he would have wished to promote
the articles of 1585, passed by Convocation and confirmed by the Queen on March 31, even without all the
pother in Parliament. They provided, first of all, for
strict standards of life and learning in ordinands, with
loss of power to ordain, for two years, by any bishop
who relaxed the standards, and for the protection of
bishops who refused to admit to livings unsuitable
persons presented by patrons. Commutation of
penance was to be allowed, solely by the bishop
himself, only for rare and serious causes, with public
confession of sin if it had been notorious. Licences to
marry without banns were carefully delimited, excommunication might only be pronounced by a lay
official if he were assisted by a cleric, livings might not
be held in plurality if they were above thirty miles
apart, and a suitable curate had to be provided; a table
of fees, not greater than those at the beginning of the
reign, was to be openly displayed in each consistory

court. Finally, the bishops were to make enquiry about all the ministers in their dioceses—their learning, their character, their ordination, etc.—and make a return to the Archbishop within a year, together with a list of all livings and their value, and even of the stipends paid to curates. Whitgift was far too fair a man to be indifferent to justifiable complaints merely because they were combined with puritan designs which he abominated. These articles of 1585 were a genuine attempt to meet them. And, though the "exercises", which the puritans wanted and the Queen did not, could not be restored, Convocation did issue orders to try to improve unlearned ministers—daily services were to be read as ordered by the rubrics, every week those who were not M.A.s or preachers were to study and analyse in Latin a chapter of the Bible assigned by the bishop, and once a quarter a "common place" of divinity was to be written on in Latin (or, at first, in English if knowledge of Latin was deficient) and the writer to be examined thereon by the bishop or some learned preacher. Those who were negligent were to be punished.

When the next Parliament met in October 1586, Whitgift's position was immeasurably stronger. He was now, since February, a member of the Council, where he could keep an eye on what was going on. In June he had been given considerable authority (along with Aylmer) over the Press. In that month orders were issued by the Star Chamber for the control of printing and the reduction of the number of presses. There were to be none outside London, except one each in Oxford and Cambridge, and no new printers were to be allowed even in London till the present number was reduced to satisfactory limits—and it was the Archbishop and the Bishop of London who were to decide when that limit was reached, and only then allow the Stationers' Company to license new printers, subject to the approval of the Ecclesiastical Commission. Moreover, save for certain specified exceptions, no books were to be printed unless allowed by the Archbishop or the Bishop of London. Though it is true that these orders were evaded, and illicit presses continued secretly to produce books and pamphlets, such powers did give Whitgift wide rights of initiative; and illicit presses were liable to be confiscated and destroyed if discovered by the agents of the Stationers' Company who had unrestricted powers to search for them. Moreover, when the Parliament met, the Queen did not appear in person but acted through a commission consisting of the Archbishop, Lord Burghley and the Earl of Derby; Whitgift could hardly have asked for any more significant advertisement of his position. Besides, the Queen, perhaps emboldened by the outburst of loyal enthusiasm released by the discovery and suppression of Babington's conspiracy, seems to have been more ready than before openly to interfere against members of the Commons who ignored her instructions. There is no evidence that Whitgift needed to call on her for help : she herself acted without his prompting. Thus, in all ways, the Archbishop was much more happily placed than he had been two years previously.

In his opening speech to Parliament, the Chancellor declared that the Queen had not summoned Parliament to make laws "whereof her Majesty thought there were more made than duly observed", but for advice about one already condemned but not yet punished. The reference was obvious. Mary, Queen of Scots, had been found guilty, by a commission specially appointed under the Great Seal to try her, of complicity in the Babington plot and of claiming the throne of England. The Queen was obviously really at a loss, convinced of Mary's guilt, but most reluctant to put her to death. The matter occupied the attention of both Houses till the adjournment on December 2—so much so that in that period no public or private bill was discussed in the Lords and only unimportant bills in the Commons. Though the Queen urged the Lords to consider if some course other than proceeding to the extremity of execution would not suffice, both Houses agreed, unanimously, that there was no other way, and petitioned for execution. The Queen replied that she could not answer Yes or No—"I must deliver you an answer answerless". But on December 4, just after the adjournment, a proclamation was made declaring the judgment of the Commission and of Parliament and stating that the sentence on Mary should be carried out. She was executed on February 8, 1587—though whether, in the end, the Queen actually meant the execution to take place is still a matter of question.

When Parliament reassembled, the problem of Mary of Scotland out of the way, it could give its mind to other matters. Despite warnings, the irrepressible puritans tried again. A certain Mr. Cope presented a bill containing a petition that all the laws in force touching ecclesiastical government should be made void and that a Book of Common Prayer which he produced should alone be authorised. There was much discussion, but in the end Cope's motion seems to have been talked out. We have neither the bill nor the book. But if Strype is right in attributing to this occasion a speech he records fully, it was a remarkably glaring attempt at innovation. The minister would not have needed to say the Prayer Book services daily, and repeatedly was given the choice of using the set prayers or something "the like in effect"; "all or the most part is left to the minister's spirit". Moreover, a full presbyterian machinery would have been established, with parish patronage in the hands of elders to whose "censures, reprehensions, suspensions and excommunications" even the Queen would be subject. The bill was not read, but the Queen was roused : she sent for the bill and book, and its proposer and his supporters (no doubt at her instigation) were interviewed by the Council and sent to the Tower; as was also Mr. Wentworth who raised questions about the privileges of

Parliament. And, though a petition was proposed to be made to the Queen for the release of the imprisoned members, Hatton seems to have had little difficulty in persuading the House not to proceed with it. It is possible that we should date here a petition sent by some of the Commons to the Queen in support of the new platform. At least there is a reply from her to some such a petition politely but firmly rejecting any further changes, saying that such constant suggestions undermine the strength of the church, that if things are amiss it is for the clergy to amend them, and that such a petition was against the prerogatives of the Crown.

Thus died out the last open and direct attempt in an Elizabethan parliament to abolish or neutralize the Book of Common Prayer and to change the established orders of clergy. Henceforward, puritan attacks there were virtually confined to attacking what they could represent as abuses, not the essence, of the system. It was a victory for Whitgift's policy (or perhaps one should say the Queen's policy—though in fact they entirely agreed) now brought about without his having to fight publicly for it. The only acts passed by Parliament which touched on religion were one for "the speedy and due execution" of the previous act to Retain the Queen's Subjects in Due Obedience, providing for stricter enforcement of the penalties for recusancy, and one confirming the subsidy of the clergy voted in Convocation. What is most significant, as a sign of growing confidence, is that the Convocation which was meeting simultaneously with Parliament was able to direct its attention in the main to the domestic rather than the political concerns of the church. Beside the matter of the subsidy, and an extraordinary benevolence to the Queen (accompanied by a strong statement of clerical poverty), there was consideration of what ordinations or institutions of unworthy persons had been made by bishops since the articles of 1585; and of complaints from Norfolk and Suffolk, the former seemingly against traditional customs still followed, the latter against innovations. Perhaps the most important measure was the acceptance by Convocation of new rules for promoting a learned and diligent clergy, insisting on study for those who were not M.A.s or licensed preachers, on supervision of such study by episcopally nominated examiners, and on the regular catechizing of the youth of the parishes by the clergy. These rules are explicitly attributed to the initiative of Whitgift, who had perhaps found that the procedure suggested in 1585 was impracticable. They are further proof, if any is needed, of his unceasing anxiety to raise, in every way practically possible, the standard of clerical learning and of pastoral care in the parishes.

There are indications that Whitgift was now, little by little, relaxing his rigour against any but really tiresome puritan ministers—possibly because he was already feeling the strength of his position backed by the Queen. Despite the violent charges of his opponents, he was really a man of peace. He was not, it is true, prepared to give way over principles, nor to appease his critics because they were influential. But equally he was anxious not to drive the puritans into extremes by unnecessary provocation (a trait which he showed strongly in 1593), and there was no trace of vindictiveness in his dealings. In all seriousness he once told Burghley that he was more afraid that he might be justly taxed with too much rather than too little tolerance. His treatment about now of Cartwright was typical. After a long sojourn abroad, the puritan leader returned in 1586 and was made by Lord Leicester the Master of his new hospital at Warwick. Whitgift welcomed him back so kindly that even Leicester wrote to express his appreciation. But he also made a request that Cartwright should be given a licence to preach—a request which Whitgift, despite its source, refused to grant (very wisely, as events proved) "until he might be better persuaded of his conformity". Personal kindness to an old and bitter opponent was there, but wise caution as well. On the other hand, he did persuade Cartwright not to publish his answer to the English translation of the Bible made by the Romans at Rheims : it would, no doubt, have provoked the recusants still more, which Whitgift wished to avoid.

Some time about now, too (the exact date is not given), he took part in a conference at Lambeth to discuss objections to the Prayer Book in a friendly manner and without the fear of judicial proceedings to check freedom of speech. It was done at Leicester's suggestion, and Lord Grey was there, and Walsingham and for part of the time Burghley, as it were to oversee the discussion. Whitgift, supported by the Bishop of Winchester and the Archbishop of York, devoted two days to it. Of the two objectors, one was his old and embittered antagonist Travers, to whom apparently our account of the meeting is due. All the usual points were raised—the reading of the Apocrypha to the neglect of canonical Scriptures; private baptism, even by women, in case of urgency; the interrogation and signing with the cross at baptism; the private communion of the sick, clerical apparel, non-preaching ministers. Walsingham, on the whole, seemed to side with Travers, Burghley with Whitgift. There was no agreement or practical result; but that Whitgift should consent to such a conference—and at Lambeth—and spend so long over it shows how anxious he was to prevail if possible by reason rather than by compulsion.

When, in 1585, Walsingham agreed to join in opposing actual breakers of order, Whitgift also forbore to require subscription to his three articles from all the clergy, and required it only from those about to be ordained or to enter on a living, being content that others should undertake to use the Prayer Book according to usage and the law, an obviously conciliatory move. Even so he needed to be very careful. On one occasion he had to point out to Walsingham that the undertaking given by a man he favoured was so worded as to be completely elusive and thus worthless. None the less, it is notable that in his visitation articles for the diocese of Chichester in 1585 there is no enquiry whether each minister had actually subscribed the three articles of 1583; all that was sought to know was whether he used the Prayer Book services and no other, whether those who preached also ministered the sacraments, whether the clerical apparel was duly worn in church and out, whether the minister instructed the youth of the parish and reminded the churchwardens to levy fines on non-attenders at the Sunday services, whether he had spoken against the Prayer Book or Articles of Religion, whether he was resident, whether he was a man of good life and so on. Surely that is reasonable enough : the Archbishop wanted to be sure that the clergy were in fact conforming and he did not seek to explore their private views. But he did also ask whether they or any other kept "any exercise of expounding, or read any lecture in private houses whereunto other, beside those of that family, do resort".

As in 1583, he was still suspicious of "conventicles" or prophesyings. And there is also in these articles a very clear authoritative reference to what was becoming a burning question—was the minister "ordered according to the laws of this realm"? So far there had not been any official pronouncement that those ordered in the protestant churches abroad were incapable of holding livings in England. Indeed, in 1571 Parliament had passed an act allowing ministers not ordained according to the book of Edward VI or Elizabeth to hold livings, provided that, before Christmas following, they subscribed to the Articles of 1561. The act was mainly intended to cover those who, under Mary, had received Roman orders but had continued under Elizabeth to serve in the Church of England; in fact, it also covered such Englishmen as had in exile been made ministers overseas. The time-limit was important; it suggested a temporary provision to avoid confusion and hardship, not the permanent authorisation of non-Anglican orders simply on condition of subscription to the Articles. That was a matter not yet decided.

The outstanding dispute so far had been with Whittingham who, without English orders, had been Dean of Durham. Sandys as Archbishop began to take steps to oust him, but Whittingham died before the issue was settled. The question was revived in 1584. The Mastership of the Temple was vacant; it was almost a key post, as many lawyers who formed the congregation were inclined to puritanism. For some years, Travers had been Reader or afternoon-lecturer there, with the approval of the Bishop of London : the late Master had suggested him as successor, some of the Benchers petitioned for him, and Burghley strongly backed his claims. Whitgift firmly opposed : he had known Travers at Trinity College, and was aware how strongly he was opposed to the existing organization of the Church of England. Later on, as the disagreement developed, Whitgift took his stand firmly on the ground that Travers had not been ordained according to the law of the land. Travers argued that, having once been made a minister, he could not be ordained again, and referred to the act of 1571 without, however, any reference to the time-limit. Whitgift firmly stood his ground. He pointed out that the act of 1571 did not in fact cover Travers. Anyhow, the case was different, for he "misliking the order of his country, ran to be ordered elsewhere, by such as had no authority to ordain him, to the contempt of the ministry of this church, and the manifest maintenance of schism". That was the simple truth : Travers had deliberately sought presbyterian orders abroad because of his dislike of episcopacy. His position was therefore different from that of the Marian clergy or even from that of those who in exile in Mary's reign had been made ministers. His was a special case—and Whitgift prevailed. Richard Hooker was made Master in 1585.

That did not settle the principle involved, and, as is well known, was not the end of the troubles at the Temple church. The Benchers voted that Travers should be continued as afternoon lecturer, with the result that "the forenoon sermon spake Canterbury, the afternoon Geneva". Moreover, the afternoon congregations were larger than the morning ones. Travers was an eloquent as well as a very sincere preacher, whereas Hooker's doctrine had "nothing but itself to garnish it". Travers even drew up a list of what he regarded as Hooker's errors, to which Hooker replied. The controversy is of interest as showing, not only the complete Calvinism of Travers, but also the much broader and more gentle views of Hooker, who maintained that the church of Rome was a true church, that those who had lived in it might be saved, that predestination was not absolute but conditional, and that reprobates are condemned for their evil works, of which God is not the author. Hooker therein showed signs of the greatness and reasonableness to be more fully displayed in the *Ecclesiastical Polity*. But such teaching, in fact, involved the rejection of the harsher points in strict Calvinism—and Travers was bitterly hostile. Called upon to give his judgment, Whitgift was in a difficulty. He was more of an administrator than a theologian, and though he cordially rejected Calvinistic church order, he hardly seems to have meditated deeply on the Calvinistic theology which was accepted almost without challenge by many English protestants at the time. He did not, of course, support Travers; but he was content rather to criticise the exaggerations of his statements than to come down very forcefully on Hooker's side. In the end, after long arguments between Hooker and Travers (carried out with complete seemliness and dignity), the latter was forbidden by the Archbishop to preach. He appealed to the Queen and Privy Council (where he had strong friends) but without success. For a few more years he stayed on in London, but was then appointed Provost in 1595 of Trinity College, Dublin.

Though it was his seeking of foreign orders which Whitgift urged against Travers most strongly, and though Whitgift prevailed, there does not seem to have been as yet any formal decision that such orders were inadequate for office in the Church of England. That was not legally enacted till the time of Charles II. There is little doubt that such ministers were to be found holding livings here and there even in the later years of Elizabeth. But by 1585 Whitgift, in his visitations, was evidently trying to identify them—perhaps spurred thereto by his troubles with Travers, though those had not yet actually come to a head.

Many other duties, too, kept Whitgift busy. Not only was his metropolitical visitation still continuing (through commissions, of course; but still the responsibility was his), but he was directly in charge of such dioceses as had no bishops—and there were five of them in 1584. He pressed Burghley to move the Queen to fill them, but received the damping reply that there seemed to be much worldliness in those that came to cathedral churches, as though the places altered the men! Nor was Whitgift, honest man, able completely to deny the charge—"I will not justify all, neither yet many of them". But he did think that circumstances were to blame rather than the men themselves, a view which impartial consideration of the age goes far to justify. Still, the vacant dioceses were a real care for him. Even where there was a bishop, Whitgift might have to intervene. The Bishop of Exeter had to clear himself against an information against him under fifteen heads. On the whole, he comes out pretty well; he had even gaoled his own son for being "seduced by a Jesuit" after he had been given a living! Such cases, however, even when only inspired by malice, must have been tiresome.

And some of the bishops were slack. The Bishop of Lincoln had to be stirred up to send in the list, ordered by Convocation, of those he had ordained and their qualifications, and a little later to see that the churches in his diocese were duly furnished with Bibles as authorised by the bishops. That is, of course, the Bishops' Bible of 1568.

Another matter calling for constant care was the protection of the clergy. They were not well off—as he wrote, in 1585, to Burghley "every waterman on the Thames earneth more by his labour than the greater part of several ministers in England do by their benefices". It is said that in 1600, in the diocese of Lichfield, 51 incumbents had less than £5 a year, 124 between £5 and £10, 30 between £10 and £15, and only 24 more than £15. They were liable for the payment of first-fruits and tenths, of subsidies, and even occasionally of special benevolences. Those who were better off were expected to provide men and arms for the Queen's service, and were constantly looked to for help in charitable causes—as when a town suffered heavily through a fire. Yet there were constant attempts to squeeze still more money from them by concealers and so on. Whitgift had to write to the Queen in 1584 to protect one of his incumbents from being wrongfully dispossessed by laymen. He had to write to Burghley to oppose (successfully) a plan to revalue all ecclesiastical livings. If it were fairly done, he was convinced that it would be found that most of them were not worth as much as they were assessed at—but he did not think it would be fairly done. The following year (1585) he had to oppose—again to Burghley and again successfully—a plan to farm out first-fruits and tenths which would, no doubt, have led to very severe handling of the clergy by greedy and probably unscrupulous speculators. Whitgift was honestly concerned about clerical poverty : he had a heart as well as a head, a fact which is sometimes overlooked. When he argued—

as he often did—that pluralism was necessary to provide adequate remuneration for able men, he was not merely putting up a dishonest defence of an abuse. He was genuinely trying to raise the clergy from the condition of a depressed class. He even took measures to maintain the "privilege of clergy" which had survived from pre-Reformation days.

The impression one gets is not only of a life busy with large matters of state and policy, but of incessant watchful care for righteousness and just dealing. He recovered for the Hospital of Eastbridge, of which he was patron, lands which had been taken from it by concealers, and then obtained an act of Parliament to settle its benefits permanently on a more generous scale. On various counts he was called in to help both Oxford and Cambridge in their difficulties, on one occasion even encouraging a college of which he was visitor to refuse a lease of woods to an applicant strongly supported by the Queen. In a remarkably short time he rescued the Primacy from the unfortunate effects of Grindal's impotence. Now at least the Archbishop was a force to be reckoned with—and a force on the side of justice in everyday things.

Chapter Ten

The Presbyterian Movement
and Marprelate

IN the fifteen-eighties there was spreading a movement, especially in the eastern and midland counties,
which aimed at the sheer presbyterianizing of the
Church of England. In itself that is not surprising.
Many of the puritans were honestly convinced that
such a form of church government was the only one
legitimately allowed by Scripture; they were too conscientious to rest with matters as they were. On the
other hand, most of them were equally certain that
it was really wrong to secede and form separatist congregations. The only possible course was therefore to
try to contrive that their views should be made effective
in the national church. Some of them, possibly, were
very young and ill-informed; some certainly were
narrow; but it is less than just not to recognise that they
were utterly sincere. What is surprising is not what
they did, but that they were so long allowed to do it,
apparently unchecked, by an autocratic government.
Probably their immunity was due to several factors.
In those years, whatever may have been the feelings of
the Queen, the Council was much more afraid of the
Roman than of the puritan danger, and was anxious
not to alienate staunch protestants. Then their meetings were not public, official, well known, but in
private houses; and those who attended them were
bound by promise to keep all their doings secret.
Finally, it is almost certain that they were in fact

doing nothing actually illegal in holding their meetings. No doubt some of their discussions and decisions were highly undesirable from the Queen's point of view; but the members always maintained that they had done nothing illegal and, as they had taken and been guided by legal advice, it is likely that their claim was justified. Though the "prophesyings" had been stopped by the bishops at the Queen's command, there was no law which forbade men to meet together to discuss religious matters. Such puritans as were dealt with by the bishops or the Commission were men who had openly attacked the Prayer Book or notoriously refused to obey it—but then those were legal offences.

In view of the secrecy of the meetings, it is natural that most of what we know about them comes from hostile sources. The chief of these is *Dangerous Positions and Proceedings published and practised within this Iland of Brytanie under Pretence of Reformation and for the Presbyterian Discipline,* by Richard Bancroft, published in 1593. He was an able man in middle life, already marked out for advancement—chaplain to Lord Keeper Hatton, Canon of Westminster and prebendary of St. Paul's, secretary and, since 1592, chaplain to Whitgift, whom he succeeded as Archbishop in 1604, after seven years as Bishop of London. He is definitely a hostile witness, violent and prejudiced perhaps, but too clever to be dishonest or invent evidence. Anyhow, he was certainly well informed. He had been the chief agent in tracking out the movement and had possessed himself of letters and documents of the leaders of it which he quotes generously and convincingly. Moreover, a good deal of what he says is more or less confirmed in the still extant record of the interrogations of puritans in the early nineties, and by the minute book of one of the "meetings" at Dedham in Essex, a most revealing document. From all these sources a fairly reliable picture can be drawn of what was going on.

Apart from a few really separist conventicles to be found in London about 1569, the first definite information we have is of a fully-fledged Presbytery at Wandsworth, complete with eleven elders and rules for their appointment and approval. They were not separatist : they explicitly declared that they would not willingly leave the Church of England despite its many faults. The document describing their organization was endorsed as "the Order of Wandsworth" by Field, one of the authors of the *Admonition* and a main promoter of the movement. Bancroft dates it as 1572, but the date is not certain. He himself admits that he cannot tell how it was "so far gone" so early. Certainly there is no known parallel to it at that time anywhere else. So far as we can gather, the general movement came later, subterranean, spontaneous, local, rising after the suppression of the prophesyings. Ministers of neighbouring churches who had become drawn to each other by similar views continued to meet privately in what they termed "fasts", at first for purely religious purposes. Then the meetings, still of members of contiguous parishes, were enlarged so as to include selected laymen, and their scope widened to cover control, or at least criticism, of the conduct of the members and discussions, not only about the Prayer Book and subscription to Whitgift's articles, but about wider issues of church polity. To such meetings about the year 1583 the term "classis" was applied. There grew up also the custom of consulting other classes on disputed points, especially the one in London, where Field occupied a central position, keeping in touch by correspondence with many parts of the country. Out of such contacts rose the idea of the classis as a member of a wider association, not a mere independent unit. The keen leaders of the movement were not slow to take advantage of this unifying tendency.

About 1583 a meeting, probably in London or Cambridge, passed certain decrees wherein (as Fuller charm-

ingly puts it) we can see "the embryo of the Presbyterian Discipline lying as yet (as it were) in the wombe
of Episcopacy". The scheme was ingenious. No one
was to seek the ministry unless called by a particular
church; then if the local classis of neighbouring districts approved, such a one was to be sent to the bishop
with letters of commendation for ordination—a neat
combination of congregationalism, presbyterianism and
episcopacy. Similarly, churchwardens and collectors
for the poor were to be quietly transformed into elders
and deacons, chosen after long notice and with due
ceremony and admonition, and received into their
"ministry" amid the prayers of the church. Even Bancroft admits that the framers of the scheme were careful not to break the peace of the church. It was agreed
that the Thirty-nine Articles so far as they concerned
only the faith and the sacraments (which was all Parliament had required) might be signed. The other articles,
about ecclesiastical matters, and the Prayer Book as a
whole, however, should not be accepted, even though
the result was deprivation. "Popish" ceremonies should
be omitted, though if such omission led to danger of deprivation, the classis should be consulted as to what was
to be done. There followed references to county and
provincial meetings and to a national assembly to be
held whenever Parliament met. In particular, when a
living was vacant, the classis was to press the patron to
present to it a "fit" man. Though obviously the whole
spirit of the decrees was really opposed to that of the
church established, it is difficult to see anything illegal
in them save possibly the advice to ignore some of the
Prayer Book ceremonial (which anyhow was already
widely done) and to refuse the subscription to the
Prayer Book which, however, puritans maintained that
Whitgift had no right to demand.

About now, Travers produced a new book, to be distinguished from *The Full and Plain Declaration* of
1573. This, the *Disciplina Ecclesiae sacra ex Dei Verbo*

descripta, was a succinct handbook in Latin for the
complete organisation of the movement but following
rather than giving rise to it, attempting to force into a
rigid mould what was spontaneous and inchoate. For
several years it was circulated, discussed, amended. It
is doubtful whether it was ever finally accepted or put
in operation, but it certainly presented a model on
which the classes and assemblies tried to model themselves. There is extant a proposed form of subscription
which declares it to be "essential and necessary for all
times" and "agreeable to God's most holy word" ex-
cepting for some few points; as that "which we desire
to be established in this church" and which subscribers
would strive "by humble suite unto her Majesty's
honourable Council and the Parliament, and by all
other lawful and convenient means to further and advance, so far as the laws and peace and the present
estate of our church will suffer it and not enforce to
the contrary". Once again the desire to do nothing
illegal is clear.

The scheme is frankly congregational. All churches
are equal and independent, all the ministers of the
several churches in their own order are equal, to be
called, tried and elected to their charge. There are to
be ministers of the word (either pastors or doctors),
elders who are to be responsible for overlooking the
lives of the members, and deacons who are to care for
the poor. Each church must have a presbytery, presided over by the minister, to look after its affairs and
to exercise discipline by admonition, suspension or excommunication, though the consent of the church as a
whole is needed for the last. So much is regarded as
simply scriptural. There follows a long section on
"synodical discipline" for which scriptural warrant is
not claimed : it is derived from the "use of the
churches". There are full directions for the meetings,
first of a classis, then of larger meetings. A provincial
synod is to consist of two ministers and two elders from

each of its twenty-four constituent classes; it is to meet every six months or oftener. A national synod, to be called when required, is to deal with the common affairs of all churches—doctrine, discipline, cere-monies. There are careful rules for procedure, espe-cially in administering censures. Though no church has any right or authority over another, the individual churches ought to obey the sentence of the majority of churches on any point if it is agreeable to the word of God.

How widely the scheme was formally accepted by subscription it is not possible to say. Certainly it was never effectively put in use as a whole. But there is plenty of evidence of attempts to make at least some of the changes it advocates. For example, in 1582 a certain Robert Wright, chaplain to Lord Rich, a very keen supporter of the movement, was in trouble. His case is interesting. What started it was that he spoke against keeping the Queen's Day—her accession day, now widely celebrated—because he said it was to make her an idol. She was annoyed—and he was brought be-fore his bishop and the Commission. There all sorts of charges were brought against him, among others that not being licensed to preach he had done so in the household of Lord Rich and that he had been chosen as chaplain there by the "flock and congregation". The case looks clear—but his defence shows how diffi-cult it was to prove illegality. He pointed out that he had not preached publicly, but only as "a private man to do them some good till they might have a sufficient pastor". As to his election, so called, his account was that Lord Rich, thinking his household more likely to listen to one they had approved in advance, had as-sembled them to ask if they could show any reason for his life or otherwise, why Wright should not be their teacher. From what we know of Lord Rich and his views, it is not reasonable to doubt that there really was a sort of congregational election (and that of a man not in Anglican orders). But, as Wright explained it, who was to say that it was illegal? The result of it all is not known, but it looks as though there would have been no trouble at all if he had not stirred the Queen's anger on another point.

There is a hint of an attempt at some such procedure even at the Temple by the ingenious Travers. He had already, under the late Master, tried to introduce innovations—that men should walk up to the table to receive communion and then pass on, neither kneeling nor sitting; and that collectors and sidesmen, unknown hitherto in that church, should be appointed, no doubt really to act as deacons and elders. In neither attempt did he succeed. When Hooker was made Master, the evening before his first sermon Travers and "two other gentlemen joined with him in the charge of this church . . . though not in the same kind of charge with him" (they look like privately appointed elders) came and suggested to him that he should not preach till notice of his appointment had been given to the congregation, so that their "allowance" might "seal" his calling. Once more, it was an attempt to get something like popular election, foiled this time by Hooker's perfectly courteous rejoinder that where such a custom prevailed he would respect it, but that where it did not he certainly would not be responsible for starting it.

Most clearly, the mode of growth and operation of the new "discipline" emerges in the minute book of the classis at Dedham in Essex (in the diocese of London). It was started in October 1582, with 13 members, and continued to meet until 1589, when it stopped partly because of complaints to the Bishop of London, but chiefly because of the death or departure of some of the "brethren". At first the chief business was to be Scripture study in private houses appointed beforehand, with a chosen speaker and moderator. Time was also allowed for deciding "profitable questions" if any were propounded. Some of the days were to be spent in prayer and fasting, and then admonition might be administered to any of the brethren touching ministry, doctrine or life. There is here no attempt at a "presbytery", but only at something like a "prophesying", and the proceedings were to be kept secret. But the range of matters considered—though often not formally "decided"—shows how widely the classis was really trying to exercise a practical control of which the law knew nothing. There were long discussions about Sabbath observance, and frequent consideration of the filling of cures—whether a brother should leave his place, or accept a "call" (including one case where the acceptance of a call was approved but another man appointed to the living : it looks as though the "call" had not come from the patron but from some unofficial parishioners). No doubt it could all be represented as mere advice, but in fact it was an attempt to control patronage. They decided that if any were asked to subscribe to Whitgift's articles, delaying tactics should be used : later, advised by the lawyers that the oath offered by the bishops was not to be allowed, they explicitly advised that subscription should not be made. Asked whether men should continue to preach though forbidden by the bishop, they deferred the matter, though, cautiously, they asked those who posed the question to produce reasons why they should disobey the bishop.

But more dangerous questions were also raised—though not always "dealt in"; how far the Prayer Book might be used; whether summonses to appear before ecclesiastical courts must be obeyed and whether in fact bishops were to be tolerated—a matter (again cautiously) "not dealt in". But they did decide that the surplice was not to be yielded to. Constantly it was resolved to find out what other churches had decided, or representatives were appointed to go to synods in London or Cambridge : attempts were made to see that, on special occasions, their "fasts" synchronised with those of other churches. So the tendency to unifying showed itself. Quite early it was agreed to make a list of ministers in the neighbourhood who were unsatisfactory for life or doctrine. And there are constant references which show that attempts were being made (which often were plainly resented) to discipline the laity : one man, for example, asked what he was to do since he had warned his people to come and be examined before a Communion service, and they just had not come.

This actual record shows how very far the classis was from attempting to put into practice the whole of the scheme of Travers and, on the whole, what great care was taken to keep within the law—though the whole spirit of the meeting was for changing the existing organization, with a strong inclination to disobedience if it could safely be practised. The same is true of the larger synods, which were meeting with increased frequency. In London in 1586 "they were of opinion" that the calling and jurisdiction of bishops was unlawful, and that the discipline should be taught "as a part of the Gospel". This, however, was not officially "concluded", but only showed as "private opinion"! There are notices of other synods, too—at Cambridge, at Ipswich, at Coventry, where Cartwright was the moving spirit. It was again decided that the episcopate was unlawful, that those deprived by bishops should not leave their cures till forced to do so, and that the discipline was to be taught as occasion offered but not to be put in use till men were better instructed in it. Up to this point, the movement was obviously growing in strength, in unity and in determination to effect changes—but still, legally. It was firmly opposed to the separatist Brownists or Barrowists.

How deep or widespread was the general backing it received in the country at large it is impossible to assess with any certainty. The evidence of the Dedham book shows that, even where there was a keen minister, the parishioners were often not amenable. Moreover, the rapidity with which the whole scheme seems to have collapsed once the authorities took action suggests that it had no very great hold on the country as a whole. At first, apparently, it was not interfered with. But in February 1589 Bancroft attacked it in a sermon in "Parliament-time" at Paul's Cross. Then the authorities acted strongly. In about three years' time after that it seems simply to have died out—which does not suggest that it had much popular support. Probably at most not more than a thousand ministers were favourers of the movement; we have knowledge only of a few hundred. But they had the zealous help of some influential laymen, such as Lord Rich, who were of great assistance, because they had the patronage of many livings, and could present to them ministers who shared their views. Outside London, where Field and Travers were leaders, they were most strong in Northamptonshire, in Warwick, in Essex, in Cambridge, in Oxford, in East Anglia. Elsewhere, though they are mentioned as existing, they were almost insignificant. Even in the districts where they were most active, there is little evidence that they had much favour with the average layman, and some to suggest the reverse. Had they been allowed to continue and grow, they might through their keenness have proved a real danger to the Established Church. As it was, authority intervened, no doubt inspired by Whitgift and Bancroft, before they had a wide hold.

Oddly enough, it looks as though it was the Marprelate tracts which first provoked episcopal enquiry and opposition, although many of the serious puritan leaders disapproved of those tracts just as much as Whitgift and Bancroft. The first tract was printed in the autumn of 1588, the last about a year later. Of course, the mere printing without authority in itself was totally illegal and heavy penalties were likely in case of discovery. That serves to emphasize the courage and persistence of the producers as they moved the press from place to place. Not only ingenuity was needed, but a high degree of fearless enthusiasm. Who actually wrote the tracts is a mystery which has never been solved.

The ostensible cause was the publication of a *Defence of the Government Established* by Dr. Bridges, Dean of Salisbury; but all through, the real driving power was an immense and impatient irritation against the bishops because they were regarded as the sole or chief obstacles to further measures of reform. In the first tract, in particular, scholarly or theological points take but small space compared with bitter abuse of individual bishops and the exposure of their (alleged) scandalous behaviour. Aylmer, of London, was especially attacked—he swore, he played bowls on Sunday —the puritans were already very touchy about Sabbath observance—he had cut down the elms at Fulham and pocketed the proceeds. There were more serious charges, too, of dishonesty and of ordaining unsuitable men. No doubt he was an easy target. In his early days he had written against episcopal pride and large incomes, whereas now he was undoubtedly avaricious; and he had been especially hard, even tyrannical, towards the ministers in his diocese who did not fully conform. Other bishops were attacked, too, in no light terms, including Whitgift, who was accused of pride and of regarding himself as the second person in the realm, of favouring papistry and of harsh treatment of puritans such as Wigginton—though not even Marprelate was able to rake up against the Archbishop any suggestion of peculation or dishonesty.

The object of the first tract seems to have been so to belabour and shatter the bishops as to frighten them into changing their policy. Though it is claimed that they cannot supervise their scattered flocks properly, yet Martin promises to refrain from further attacks if they will cease their persecutions and their insistence on subscription to Whitgift's articles, ordain suitable men and promote preaching—in fact, not press the points to which the puritans objected. If they will not come to terms so, he threatens most violently : he will set spies everywhere and disclose all their doings.

Whitgift was not the man to be diverted by such methods from what he thought to be his duty. He conferred with other bishops and arranged for a reply to Martin's attack. It appeared in January, edited by Cooper, Bishop of Winchester—*An Admonition to the People of England*—containing answers by individual bishops to the charges Martin had brought against them. The defence is undoubtedly neither so lively nor such good reading as Martin's attack, but at least it is sufficient to shake one's confidence in his strict accuracy. Whitgift had little difficulty in clearing himself : much of what Martin had said about him simply was not true, and the rest was maliciously twisted. Even Aylmer was able to argue that all he had done had been strictly legal (though he still emerges as a rather greedy person) and so on. When mud has been removed, however, stains which are ineradicable are apt to remain, and Martin's attack did permanently affect episcopal reputations. Much of what he said was doubtless exaggerated and malicious, or even false. But the bishops were not, at least all of them, saints. Some were ambitious, covetous, at times hard and tyrannical. In 1584 Aylmer was actually warned by the Council to pay compensation to an incumbent he had kept in prison for five years, for if a case were presented in the courts for wrongful imprisonment, it would undoubtedly succeed against the bishop. In view of such things, folk were more willing on very slight evidence to believe in episcopal enormities than to be convinced, even by the best of proofs, that the bishops were faultless.

Before Cooper's *Admonition* appeared, however,

Martin had wind of what the bishops were doing, and issued his second tract. He now moved on to the ground which was henceforward to provide his main standing. "The whole controversy", he maintained, concerned the question whether the external government of the church was a matter so "prescribed by the Lord in the New Testament" as to be not lawful for any man to alter. He is quite sure not only that there was, but that there must be, such an order : to deny it is "so mad and wicked as to say that our Saviour Christ left behind Him, here on earth, an unperfect and maimed body", as he says in a later tract. There is henceforward no suggestion of a compromise with episcopacy, but frank and violent support for presbyterianism, bolstered up by telling references, given with obvious enjoyment, to Aylmer's early attacks on the bishops. Martin's arguments were not new and need not be detailed. At times they are verbose and tiresomely repetitive. What was new was the spirit of it all. The seemliness and, at least comparative, restraint of the argument between Hooker and Travers or even Whitgift and Cartwright now gave way to a violence and objurgation which were hitherto unknown in the controversy, and virulent personal attacks on individual bishops still from time to time suddenly emerged.

Frankly, there is much in the tracts which does not appeal to modern tastes. To refer to the Archbishop as "John Cant", or to Cooper of Winchester as "Tom Tubtrimmer" is not very subtle, and although the change of Aylmer into "Marelme" has more point, it was not Martin's own invention and stales with repetition. Nor does it now seem very funny to refer to Convocation as "Confocation" or "Conspiration" house, vicar-general as "ficker"-general, or to the Archbishop as "paltripolitan", or to address the Bishop of Winchester as "you sodden-headed ass, you"! None the less, there was a raciness and a lively vigour about the tracts which even now make them easier reading than some of the more reputable and scholarly puritan writings full of niggling points from which, possibly, a sense of humour might have saved them. And there are phrases which, whether one likes them or not, do stick. Bridges' style is "as smooth as a crab-tree cudgel"; the bishops are "impudent, shameless, wainscot-faced"; Whitgift, surely unjustly, is "past shame and a notorious liar". Indeed, nothing could prove more conclusively the force and importance of the Archbishop's position in leading and directing the opposition than the constant abuse to which he is subjected. He was plainly, in Martin's view, the villain of the piece : the church he regards as simply misled by the bishops—"proud, popish, presumptuous, profane, paltry, pestilent and pernicious". And among the bishops Whitgift was pre-eminent. Despite the torrents of mockery and vituperation it is impossible not to feel the burning indignation and serious aims of Martin.

From the very beginning, many puritans were shocked and alienated by the tone of the writings—Cartwright, for example, never approved of them. Martin himself became increasingly uneasy about their disapproval, and defended himself on the ground that "The Lord being the author both of mirth and gravity, is it not lawful in itself, for the truth to use either of these ways, when the circumstances do make it lawful?" The sober puritans were not, however, appeased. On the other hand, there seems to be little doubt that the tracts made an immediate and wide appeal to readers less strait-laced who loved a joke even if—and perhaps because—it was broad or scandalous. They were at once the talk of the day, and even members of the Court were among their readers. One point in particular must have commended them to many who in that lively age were striving for wealth or power—Martin's opposition was not merely to the episcopal order as such; he was almost beside himself at the pride and pomp of bishops. He just could not bear "lords bishop". Many in his day, even though they might not have shared his theological views, were no doubt very ready—as indeed their descendants have ever been—to take offence at what is commonly summed up as "prelacy".

Chapter Eleven

The Repression
of Non-Conformity

THE outcome of Marprelate's activity was the reverse of what he hoped. Though he tickled the worldly—Wigginton, examined in December, declared that "many Lords and Ladies and other great and wealthy personages" had copies of his work—he undoubtedly offended the real leaders of the puritan movement, and did not win serious support for it. Even Secretary Walsingham, no friend to episcopacy, was put off : Martin had gone too far. His one solid achievement was that the authorities were forced to take action. Only a month after the appearance of the first tract, the Lord Chancellor and Burghley wrote to Whitgift, at the Queen's order. She had heard of the "lewd and seditious book" secretly dispersed by persons of "unquiet spirits" containing "in a malicious spirit sundry slanderous reports". Whitgift therefore was to "use all privy means, by force of your commission ecclesiastical or otherwise" to search out the authors, printers and distributors, to apprehend and commit them. He was to report his proceedings to the Council so that due measures could be taken against the offenders. The Archbishop was not slow to move. Immediately he planned with the Bishops of London, Winchester and Lincoln the *Admonition to the People of England,* which appeared with astonishing rapidity in a few months. An even more effective step was the setting on of Bancroft to ferret out the Martinists and their friends. He was just the man for the work, untiring in his efforts, quite sure of his own views.

Bancroft quickly assessed the danger, not only of the tracts, but of the whole presbyterian movement they supported. On February 9, 1589, the first Sunday of the new Parliament, he preached at Paul's Cross his famous and unsparing attack on the innovators. In vigour, indignation, argument it was at least the equal of the Marprelate letters; its scorn and sarcasm were extremely effective and, though it was harsh and censorious, it avoided the scurrilous personalities in which Martin obviously delighted. If the intention of Christ was so clear as was alleged, Bancroft remarked, it was very odd that no church, at least after Nicaea, was organised on the lines suggested till after 1500. Only then, apparently, was the obvious teaching of the New Testament discovered. Even so, it was not quite pellucid. The new discipline book had needed revision almost yearly—and there were at least 600 alterations in it! As to their proposed Prayer Book, the minister need not strictly follow it but might pray "as the spirit of God shall move his heart"; the result was sometimes so malicious that no Christian ought to say "Amen". He was scornful of the presumptuous ignorance of some of the puritans, of the arrogance of their youthful leaders. "The prattling old woman, the doting old man, the brabbling sophister and generally all men" presume that they have "the art of the Scriptures". "One of four or five and twenty years old, if you anger him, will swear that he knoweth more than all the ancient fathers ... every boy, in a manner, doth take upon him (as though he only were learned, zealous and wise) to control, condemn and rage thus at his pleasure." Whitgift, too, had found just those qualities in some he had to deal with when first he became Archbishop. Moreover, like Whitgift, Bancroft was sickened by an apparent humility which he was convinced was the superficial covering of deep-seated pride. They "bitterly exclaim against the pride of bishops as though they affected nothing else by their desired equality but some great lowliness, and to prostrate themselves at your feet for your service; whereas indeed they shoot at greater superiority and preeminence than ever your bishops did use or challenge unto them; and would no doubt tyrannize by their censure over both prince and people at their pleasure in most intolerable and pope-like manner". Such outbursts no doubt lack the gentle tones of charity; but their justification is easy to find in the insolent—not to say impudent—bearing of some of the puritans on trial.

Bancroft had more weighty ammunition than mere dislike, disdain and derision. Martin and his followers were so cock-sure ("they think well of nothing but of that they do themselves") that they "despise government and fear not to speak evil of them that are in dignity and authority". He pointed out that logically they would soon seek to overrule the magistrates and even the Queen herself. On their argument, she was a "petty pope" in so far as she now wielded in causes ecclesiastical what had been papal powers. The point was enforced by a telling reference to Scotland, where "under the pretence of their presbyteries they trod upon the sceptre". The King's "crown and their sovereignty will not agree together". It was an argument well calculated to appeal to the Queen, whose view it undoutedly expressed. Finally, he carried the war right into the enemy's country. All that Whitgift had maintained against Cartwright was that episcopacy was at least one of the legitimate forms of church government. Bancroft virtually claimed for it apostolic authority—and he is generally supposed to be the first Anglican to do so. "Bishops have had this authority which Martin condemneth ever since St. Mark's time." "There is no man living, as I suppose, able to show where there was any church planted ever since the apostles' time, but there the bishops had authority over the rest of the ministry." "The church of God ever since the apostles' time hath distributed the ecclesiastical ministry principally into these three parts, bishops, priests and deacons." Modern scholars might not wish to go so far, though there is much virtue in that saving "principally". But at last the challenge of the puritans was firmly met—and on a ground typical of the whole character of Anglicanism. The early practice of the church as well as the mere letter of the New Testament was to be regarded as the norm for church government.

The sermon was at once a declaration of war on the presbyterianizer and a proof that the defenders of episcopacy could give blows as stout as they received. Of course Knollys, with his view that bishops drew all their authority from the Crown was very much flustered. He wrote off to Oxford to ask for comment on Bancroft's view of episcopacy. Later in the summer he tackled Burghley on the matter and, receiving but cold comfort, tried again in August, only once more to be rebuffed. For Burghley, despite his leanings towards some of the puritans and his anxiety to protect them from injustice, was not at heart a presbyterian. Nor seemingly was Secretary Walsingham. The Bishop of Durham, Dr. Hutton, had a conference in October with the two of them, Burghley arguing like "a fresh University man" on the topic of episcopacy despite all his other cares, and Walsingham showing a knowledge of divinity matters far beyond expectation. They both agreed with Hutton and treated him most honourably.

In fact, now that Marprelate had brought matters to a head, authority, so far from rejecting Bancroft's views, came down heavily on his side. Four days after his sermon there was a Royal Proclamation (February 13, 1589) expressing in unmistakable terms the Queen's dislike of the Martinist writings "in railing sort and beyond the bounds of all good humanity". They threatened not only the government of the Church, but her own prerogative : any who possessed copies were to surrender them, nor were any to handle similar effusions. Even in Parliament the puritan element, though still restless, seems to have been subdued. There was no attempt, as there had previously been, to change the Prayer Book or ecclesiastical orders : the most that was ventured was an attack on what were universally admitted to be blemishes. One member of the Commons complained that the ecclesiastical laws were not administered according to the meaning of the law makers, and offered a list of proofs. The House, reminded of the Queen's inhibition, refused to have his paper of proofs read. A bill to deal with pluralities and non-residence was produced and, re-fashioned by a committee which included such puritans as Knollys and Beale, sent up to the Lords. Even in the Commons it was strongly contested; the Lords would have nothing to do with it.

Whitgift, always on guard, was as anxious as anyone that recognised blemishes should be removed—but not by Parliament. It was apparently he who drew up arguments for those who opposed the pluralities bill; doubtless he had also much to do with framing a petition which Convocation presented to the Queen against it. There are interesting points in this petition. It was claimed that the number of learned ministers in England was now greater than in any reformed church abroad, thanks to "the benefits of your Majesty's most sacred and careful government", but it was also pointed out that, because of impropriations of tithe, the clergy were really poor, and that out of some 8,800 livings, not more than 600 were fit, held singly, to provide for learned men. Moreover—surely a very palpable hit— the bill as proposed would not affect lay impropriators who would still be able to have divers livings served by "silly curates", while it would interfere with "learned divines" who, if not resident, did at least provide "sufficient substitutes".

The bill came to nothing. But Whitgift knew quite

well that pluralities and non-residence were undesirable and was eager that they should be limited by the church itself. Unruffled by Martin's attacks, without fear that he should be accused of being bullied into making concessions, he personally presented to Convocation such rules as he thought feasible. Convocation accepted them and they were confirmed by the Queen. The holder of a single benefice must be resident, unless he had some other clerical appointment (e.g. a prebend), in which case he was to employ a "licensed, preaching curate". Those who held two benefices were to reside equally at each and provide a licensed curate in their absence. Moreover, such curates—an important point—could neither be appointed nor dismissed without the authority of the Archbishop or bishop. Further, "scandalous ministers guilty of notorious crimes" were to be removed and not given any other living. Nor was any man so unlearned as to be unable to catechize to be admitted to a cure.

The orders were an honest attempt to deal with the problem as far as was practicable at the moment. They are typical of Whitgift's steady aim to improve clerical standards and show his growing confidence, by 1589, that satisfactory clergy were, in increasing numbers, to be had. His constant efforts were evidently beginning to bear fruit. His visitation articles for his own diocese of Canterbury in the same year show his steady persistence in the same cause. Is the incumbent a preacher, and is there a monthly sermon—and are the Homilies read when there is not a sermon? Is he resident? Is he a pluralist?—and so on. None the less, though things were better than they had been, the Archbishop was not satisfied. He wrote to Burghley to complain of the state of affairs in Oxford. Lack of discipline, slackness in instruction, the too easy giving of degrees meant that the University was not providing the church with such ministers as it should. No detail seems to have escaped his vigilance in his efforts to secure a better type of clergyman.

Meanwhile, the search for the secret Martinist press was hotly pursued. As early as November 1588, enquiries had been made in Kingston about the first tract, which had in fact been printed nearby at East Molesey, in Surrey—which shows how quick on the track were the authorities. The press was secretly moved: it was at three separate places before it was finally discovered in August 1589 at a fourth near Manchester by the Earl of Derby's men. The printers were sent to London for trial. Whitgift, writing to Lord Burghley, makes the interesting comment that "in respect of myself (the greatest mote in their eye) I make small account of their malice, neither did I ever break sleep for the care thereof". But he adds that, because of the scandal caused by such lewd libels in the minds of "men apt to believe anything", he hopes they will be dealt with according to their deserts and that "rather by your lordships than by ourselves". He shows no vindictiveness nor any feeling that he need worry about his own actions, only a dispassionate wish that the bishops should be duly vindicated, which would be much better done by others than by themselves.

The captured printers were sharply questioned, even under torture, but either would not or could not give any information about the writer of the tracts. Indeed, even after they were taken, a last tract was actually printed by some means or other. But in October 1589 one Sharpe, who had been employed as binder at Northampton, made a full statement before the Lord Chancellor. From this it was clear that John Penry, if not the actual writer, was at least intimately connected with the tracts, and John Udall seemed also to be implicated. Both were already suspect. Udall, a minister at Kingston, had been deprived by the Commission in 1586 and, though restored through the intervention of influential friends, had been again deprived in 1588, whereupon he had migrated to Newcastle. Penry, too, had been before the Commission in 1587 and had engaged in violent controversy with Whitgift, though, after a month's imprisonment, he was released. The suggestion that they were connected with Marprelate did not, therefore, fall on unwilling ears. At the end of December, Udall was summoned to London to appear before the Privy Council: in January 1590 Penry's study was ransacked in his absence—he had withdrawn to Scotland—and books and papers were confiscated. No doubt it was a valuable haul, and his arrest was ordered.

Udall was examined twice before the Privy Council. Though he admitted that he thought some of Marprelate's matter was derived from his notes, he refused to say how that could have come about. Nor would he give answers which might involve other men. He also asked to be excused from answering questions about the authorship of two tracts—the *Demonstration* and the *Diotrephes*—which in fact he had himself published anonymously, attacking the established order very strongly: his reluctance to reply only strengthened the suspicion that he was the author. He was therefore sent to be tried at the Assizes at Croydon in July. Invited to deny the authorship of the *Demonstration*, he refused, and was thereupon found guilty of having published a "wicked, scandalous and seditious libel", and so liable to death under the Act of 1581 against those who published seditious words or rumours against the Queen. It does not appear to have been proved that he was the writer of the tracts; he was condemned simply because he would not deny it. He was kept in prison, and though offered his freedom if he would recant, he refused. He was tried again at the Assizes in February 1591, and was then condemned to death, but was still left in prison. Powerful friends—Raleigh, the Earl of Essex, even Nowell, Dean of St.

Paul's—worked for his release. But it was not until Whitgift intervened that the Queen granted him his life, provided that he accepted a chaplaincy in Syria, offered to him by the Turkey Company. He died in prison about the end of 1592 before the arrangements for his freedom were completed, being in his early thirties.

The Ecclesiastical Commission was not inactive in the hunt : Cartwright was summoned to appear before them on October 8, 1590. He appealed to Burghley for help, protesting that he had no connection with Marprelate, whose writings he had always condemned, and that he had not himself written anything offensive to the Queen. Burghley, though set against unfair persecution, would not interfere officially with the proceedings in the Commission. But he wrote to Whitgift to suggest that he should not personally be present among the commissioners when Cartwright appeared, and urging that he should not be "charged with old causes". He added that he saw not that diligence and care taken to win such precise men by learning or courtesy as he imagined might reclaim them. Burghley was still not happy, even now, about the proceedings of the commissioners. Whether as a result of Burghley's advice or from his own sense of·decency, Whitgift absented himself when Cartwright was tried. The Bishop of London was there, and Bancroft, supported by a strong body of legal members, the two chief justices, Justice Gawdy, Sergeant Pickering and the Attorney-General. The proceedings were evidently meant to have full legal authority and not to be swayed by mere ecclesiastical passions or personages. Cartwright, invited to take the oath *ex officio* to answer any questions put to him, refused it as contrary to the laws both of God and of the land. The questions it was proposed to put to him were then read. He still would not take the general oath, though he agreed to answer on oath such questions as concerned himself, if they were shown to him beforehand, or to give his reasons for not answering : but he firmly refused to incriminate others. The Commission still insisted on the general oath, and on his refusal (after two appearances) to take it, he was committed to the Fleet prison, some time before November 4, 1590.

The articles drawn up for him to answer were exhaustive—there were 31 in all—and certainly did not omit "old causes". They covered his ministry in the Low Countries, when he really had set up a presbytery and discipline, and had conferred orders (on Travers, among others). His doings since his return to Warwick were minutely catalogued, often with precise dates— he had preached without licence and had not desisted even when expressly forbidden by the bishop; he had spoken and acted against the Prayer Book and had encouraged others to do the same; he had attacked the episcopal government of the church. He was accused, too, of knowing but not declaring who were the authors of Marprelate, of *Diostrephes* and of the *Demonstration*, of having been instrumental in drawing up and urging subscriptions to the Discipline (of Travers) and of taking part in synods and classes in various parts of the country, of striving to set up presbyteries. Whoever drew up the questions had certainly taken the trouble to cover as wide a field as possible and to obtain exact evidence. Possibly, by now, the authorities had possession of the minute book of the Warwick classis. A year or two later, Bancroft was certainly able to make large use of it in his *Dangerous Positions*.

The imprisonment of Cartwright was a severe shock to the puritans; there were even suggestions that there might be trouble about it. In fact, nothing violent happened. In spite of his appeals that he might at least be allowed bail and his complaints to Burghley that his health was threatened by the conditions of his imprisonment, he was kept in the Fleet prison until May

1591, when he was once more brought before the Commission. The main point then at issue was the oath *ex officio*, and the argument at times was heated, even the Bishop of London at one point openly disagreeing with Bancroft. Once more Cartwright was firm; the Bishop of London thereupon irritably said he had not leisure to hear the written answers he had drawn up to the interrogatories, though Bancroft asserted that the Queen herself had seen them. The legality of requiring the oath now became a matter of heated controversy among the lawyers, but a strong committee of judges and others finally decided that it was, in fact, legal.

As he refused to take the oath, Cartwright was kept in prison and the matter was referred to the Star Chamber, where the bill of information against him rested largely on evidence supplied by Bancroft. He was examined more than once in June 1591, along with eight other prominent puritans who were now in various prisons in London. Their depositions still exist, as do also the statements of various witnesses both for and against them. In the event, no real conclusion was reached. The prisoners admitted that the Church of England, though in their view still in need of further reform, was at least such that no one need withdraw from it into schism, and that none of the clergy should make any changes, nor any synod make constitutions "without her Majesty's authority and assent". All but one of them admitted attending meetings and conferences, and that they had considered the "draught of discipline"; only five would agree that they had signed the draft, and then only as "a declaration of their judgment, leaving the determination to her Majesty and the Parliament". As to their meetings, they had simply agreed "to meet in conference, as they might by the laws of the land". The meetings were voluntary, and any decisions taken were only an expression of that "which these defendants desire to be established by public authority". Most of those who attended had not subscribed the Discipline, nor had any attempt been made to exercise authority.

It all sounded very reasonable and law-abiding. Nor did the depositions of the witnesses seriously discredit their admissions. A good deal of light was thrown on the classes and synods and what they had discussed; it was plain that there had been much criticism of the established order. Some, it was asserted, had actually agreed to a voluntary observance of the rulings of the classes in doctrine and discipline. But all the witnesses agreed that "the eldership" was not put in use. The outcome of this most searching examination of prisoners and witnesses was that the Star Chamber did not convict them. Their plans and even some of their views were no doubt highly undesirable, but they were not proved to have broken the law. Still—they were kept in prison.

They had, of course, influential friends who worked for them, such as Knollys. His sister-in-law, Lady Russell, wrote to Burghley on their behalf, and so on. In December they announced that they proposed to appeal to the Privy Council. Burghley thereupon asked the Attorney-General for his views of the whole case. His reply, as giving the legal position, is very significant. He agreed that the prisoners were resolved to have their own form of discipline generally exercised, but only "so as far as the same might be done with the peace of the church and the laws of the land". He added that some of them had resolved to try to win ministers and congregations to a voluntary acceptance of the discipline, and so generally spread its use as, really, to force the hands of the government. He did not, however, find that, as yet, they had done anything illegal. The appeal to the Council led to nothing save further questioning in which Whitgift now for the first time took a prominent part, administering the questions on behalf of the Council.

In fact, the end was in sight. By January 1592 five of the prisoners were allowed out in the day-time for their own affairs or to go to church on Sunday, though they had to return at night. Such liberty was not extended to Cartwright and the other three—but we have Cartwright's own statement that the concession was due to Whitgift. It was now becoming clear that their best hope was to obtain Whitgift's support. On Burghley's advice, Cartwright prepared an appeal to the Archbishop. Burghley also seems to have written to him. The result of Cartwright's appeal, conveyed by his wife, was that he too was allowed out of prison on Sunday and one day a week. A further appeal for full release Whitgift sent to the Attorney-General for a statement of the terms on which release was possible. When they saw the form of submission suggested, the prisoners could not in conscience sign it. Not only did it require full recognition of the Queen's authority, and of the Church of England as a true member of the Church of Christ, but it also demanded agreement that "the government challenged, devised or attempted to be executed" by any presbyteries or church assemblies of doctors, pastors, elders and deacons was not only unlawful but "very dangerous for the state of this realm"; that it was "seditious and ungodly" even to try to promote presbyteries. They inevitably refused to sign; to agree would have offended their sincere convictions. Once more there were appeals to Burghley— from leaders in Cambridge, from the prisoners themselves who pleaded for full bail till they were called for further trial. Soon afterwards they were set free— the exact date is not known, but it was before May 21, 1592. On their full acknowledgment of the royal supremacy, the Privy Council agreed that the charges of sedition and disloyalty should not be proceeded with. The matter of the oath *ex officio* seems to have been discreetly dropped.

The whole episode makes disturbing reading. Nor is

disquiet completely removed by the knowledge either that political standards in those days were very different from what they are now, or that so much consideration would probably not have been shown to dissidents in any other country, either Roman or protestant, of their day : none of them was put to death or even imprisoned for life. But the fact remains that for some eighteen months they suffered imprisonment with considerable hardships without ever being proved guilty on any charge save that of refusing the *ex officio* oath. About that they had conscientious scruples which some of the lawyers shared and with which we may well sympathize : it does not seem just that a man should be asked to answer questions, and possibly incriminate himself, on oath without any accusation being made by witnesses.

None the less, there is something to be said on the other side. The authorities, civil as well as ecclesiastical, were alarmed as to what might result from their activities. Some puritan writers had suggested steps which would have overthrown the power of the magistrates, even of the Queen; very wild things had been said by some of the hot-heads. It was not unnatural that their views should have been thought to be typical of the movement as a whole, which thus looked revolutionary. It is easy to see now that Cartwright was not the man to approve such doings : yet even he had not kept within the law at Warwick. Besides, fear of real disturbance was strengthened by what had happened in Scotland. Nor was the conduct of Hackett and his supporters likely to quieten the fears of the government. In July 1591 he proclaimed himself in London as Christ. He was mad, and met with nothing but ridicule. He was executed in July: his supporter, Coppinger, starved himself to death in prison. Before his madness was complete, however, he had been plotting to remove Queen and bishops with a view to the establishment of "the discipline". On trial, he admitted that he had declared that Elizabeth was not truly Queen. Cartwright, of course, would have nothing to do with him, but he does seem to have secured some sort of encouragement from Wigginton. The whole plot, crack-brained though it was, and without support from any sober puritan, cannot have lessened the suspicions of Elizabeth and the Council. It is not fair to forget that there were real alarms for the safety of the state : and in the end the chief puritan prisoners were released once their loyalty to the Queen and avoidance of all seditious motives were firmly assured.

In the drive against puritan leaders it is not easy to assess Whitgift's exact part. It was he who set on foot the enquiries of Bancroft which was the first move, and no doubt he was the real power, under the Queen, behind the proceedings. He obviously knew all that was going on. As early as July 1590 he sent to Burghley a long set of articles cataloguing many of the doings and views of the dissidents. The weight of his authority emerges in the fact that, both in the case of Udall and in that of the other nine, no real alleviation was possible for the prisoners till he agreed. Not even Burghley would do anything but write to the Archbishop, though there is evidence in his papers that he was well informed about everything. On the other hand, Whitgift seems to have tried to keep out of the actual trials —of Udall completely, and of Cartwright and the rest both before the Commission and, so far as is known, in Star Chamber. He did, it is true, put the questions when the trial was before the Privy Council, but there was not really anything new propounded there. The oppressive terms of the submission offered to the ministers in 1592 were drawn up not by him but by the Attorney General. It looks as though he was content to see that the cases were brought and then to have kept in the background, leaving the issue to civilians, so far as possible. In his position, he could hardly have done less.

Those who write with enthusiasm of the conscientiousness of the puritans and their courage seem sometimes
to overlook the possibility that Whitgift, too, had a conscience and needed courage to carry out its rulings. But
once satisfied that the cases were set afoot, he interfered
only to secure the release of prisoners, on their submission.

The separatists presented a problem different from
ordinary puritanism. They condemned the Church of
England outright and were unwilling to be members
of it : they wanted it to be not further reformed but
abolished. To most of their contemporaries therefore
they were just revolutionaries : Cartwright and his
friends were as strongly opposed to them as Whitgift
and the Queen. Browne and Harrison, who had been
the first leaders in Norwich, were forced to flee to the
Low Countries, where they established a congregation,
but there they quarrelled. Harrison died in 1587;
Browne returned to England, was reconciled to the
church, ordained in 1591 and presented to a living.
Still, after their flight, their followers continued to
hold surreptitious meetings, not only in Norwich but
also in London, where the tradition of such conventicles went back to the days of Queen Mary. New
leaders took the place of old—John Greenwood, who
had received orders in the Church of England and
acted as chaplain in the household of Lord Rich before
he withdrew into schism; and, even more important,
Henry Barrow who, after a dissipated youth, was converted by Greenwood and became the ablest defender
of the movement. Brownists and Barrowists—there is
no really significant difference between them—were
frankly congregationalists in the simplest sense, not
presbyterians. As they refused to attend their parish
churches, they were liable to punishment under the
act of 1581.

Even towards them, despite their general unpopularity, considerable forbearance was shown. Still, some-

thing had to be done. In the autumn of 1588 Green-wood was arrested while conducting a conventicle, and imprisoned in the Clink : Barrow, coming to visit him, was thereupon arrested as well. Before the Ecclesiastical Commission, Barrow, though professing full loyalty to the Queen, refused the supremacy oath, and declared that church reform should be pressed even against the express order of the prince whom the pastor had the right to excommunicate. He and Green-wood were subsequently examined by the civil authorities and imprisoned in the Fleet. Barrow, impenitent, spent his time in writing subversionary tracts which were printed in Holland. Other separatists were also arrested—an appeal to Burghley asking for a fair trial lists the names of 59 as being in prison and of 10 who had already died there. Learned divines, including Andrewes, were sent to argue with them but in vain. Barrow attacked the Archbishop in unmeasured terms, and summed up his insuperable objections to the Church of England—it contained all manner of evil persons and so was not pure, its ministry was unlawful, its worship superstitious and unlawful, its government anti-Christian. He and Greenwood were tried in March 1593, found guilty of seditious writings and condemned to death. After various delays they were hanged at Tyburn on April 6, but for sedition rather than for non-conformity.

About the time of their execution, Parliament, alarmed by the growth of separatism (Raleigh said their were twenty thousand of them), passed an act to deal with the situation. Those who refused to go to church or who attended illegal conventicles were to be imprisoned. If by the end of three months they did not submit, they were to abjure and leave the realm; if thereafter they returned, they were to be treated as felons. No doubt it was a very heavy punishment : but separatists were usually regarded then as not merely religious dissidents but as subversive of society—a view confirmed by Barrow's teaching. Most of those still in prison were allowed to join the London congregation in emigrating, which at least prevented a holocaust.

In 1593 one other puritan extremist was eliminated. John Penry, whose arrest had been ordered in 1590, left his security in Scotland at the end of 1592 and returned to London, where he joined a separatist group in Stepney. In March 1593 he was betrayed and arrested. Though he was widely believed to have had a great deal to do with the Marprelate tracts, and even to have been their writer, the government evidently felt that their evidence was not enough to secure a conviction on that count, and there is no mention of it in the charges against him. Nor, apparently, were his actual publications used, though in them he had not been gentle in his criticism of the Council who "delight in this injury and violent oppression of God's saints", of Whitgift "one of the dishonourablest creatures under heaven", and, by implication, of the Queen herself. Instead, the prosecution relied on some of his manuscript notes which they had found, in which the Queen was described as having turned against Christ, and ministers of church and state as being conspirators against God. Even Penry was reasoned with in prison, but to no effect. On May 21 he was condemned for having written words intended to invite rebellion and insurrection. He was argumentative to the end, and protested to Burghley that the notes did not express his real views and that, indeed, some of them had only been collected that he might reply to them. There is some doubt whether, even according to the laws of that day, his condemnation was legal. But the speed with which the sentence was carried out, contrasted with the delays over Udall, suggests that the authorities were determined to have his life if he would not recant.

Chapter Twelve

The Literary Defence of Anglicanism: Efforts to Check Abuses

THE determination shown by the government proved surprisingly effective. The non-conformists, as Fuller puts it, "began now to repose themselves in a sad silence, especially since the condemnation of Udall and Penry had so terrified them that though they might have secret designs, we meet not their open and publick motions". For the rest of Elizabeth's reign, the surviving puritan leaders were quiescent and unmolested. Cartwright, after a sojourn in Guernsey, returned to Warwick; Travers, after a brief tenure of the Provostship of Trinity College, Dublin, came back to England : both were quiet, unpersecuted, and allowed to live and die in prosperity, the latter not until 1634. Similarly, Wilcox, much respected as a spiritual adviser, died in uncontentious peace in 1608. Even Wigginton, who had nearly been compromised in the Hackett conspiracy, was allowed to return to Sedbergh and caused no more trouble. With the real leaders thus silent, the attempt to presbyterianize the church for the time being died down—which shows how little general enthusiasm it had roused, dangerous though it might have been if unchecked. For this outcome of the struggle the wisdom and courage of Whitgift deserve much of the credit. He had shown firmness, but it was tempered with moderation just at the right moment to prevent martyrdoms which might have roused fanaticism. Only separatists—for Penry at the end was such, as well as Barrow and Greenwood—had been put to death. There was very little sympathy for them. Others had suffered imprisonment, but Whitgift saw to it that (except for Udall) they were released and allowed to live unharried. He did not press his victory to extremes.

The Parliament, too, of 1593 fell in with the wishes of authority. At the opening of the session it was warned not to make new laws or even long speeches "full of verbosity and vain ostentations"; in the Commons the Queen only granted freedom of speech "in respect of Aye and No, but not that every one should speak as he listed". The chief business of the session was to provide funds to meet the dangers still anxiously expected from Spain. When, straying beyond this, certain of the Commons suggested that the Queen should settle the succession to the Crown, they were imprisoned—and the House did not dare to petition for their release. Two bills (suggested by Knollys and Beale) were proposed, one to abolish, the other to render ineffective, the *ex officio* oath. Even in the House they met with much opposition; the Queen was furious, and ordered that no such matters should be dealt with. Beale was commanded to absent himself from Court and Parliament. In the end, only two acts concerning religion were passed "to suppress the obstinate recusant and the dangerous sectary, both very pernicious", as the Speaker put it. That against the sectaries, in effect expelling them from the country, has already been noticed. That against popish recusants, in addition to the regular fines for non-attendance at church, forbade them to travel more than five miles from their accustomed place of residence. It is impossible to escape the conclusion that the government regarded separatists as a greater danger to the realm than loyal but non-conforming recusants. It is to be remembered, however, that many of the papists were wealthy and much could be got from them by fines if they stayed here. That was not true of the separatists. Both acts must have been much to the Queen's liking.

In the same year, as if to clinch the victory, Bancroft published two books not only attacking the supposed basis of the presbyterian discipline and pouring ridicule on it and its supporters, but also showing how dangerous it was to the civil as well as to the ecclesiastical government. In his *Survey of the Pretended Holy Discipline* he presented the movement as symptomatic of a general upsurge against recognised authority. A no doubt biased but none the less effective account of the methods by which Calvin achieved his authority in Geneva does not dispose the reader to regard his form of discipline as "come lately from heaven, with an embassage from God" so that all churches must conform to it. The efforts of Calvin and Beza to interfere in other countries Bancroft resents; it was more than even Pope Leo had done. He insists that the powers claimed for the elders would spread their control over the whole of men's lives and reduce the very prince to their control. He makes great play with the differing customs of the various protestant churches—"they are not thoroughly agreed in almost anything"—and with the constant need to revise the suggested discipline book. The idea that such a system was instituted by Christ and then abandoned is curtly dismissed: "all out of square from the Apostles' time till Geneva was illuminated". He firmly maintains that bishops were instituted by the apostles, and "who can be accounted to be well in his wits that will imagine that Christ should ordain such an authority but for some threescore years?" In his *Dangerous Positions and Proceedings* he is even more emphatic about the seditious tendency of the whole movement. "Ridiculous men and bewitched! As though Christ's sovereignty, kingdom and lordship were nowhere acknowledged or to be found, but where half a dozen artisans, shoemakers, tinkers and tailors, with their Preacher and Reader (eight or nine cherubins forsooth) do rule the whole parish." In Scotland, the ministers had wrought more mischief in thirty years than the Pope of Rome in five hundred. He gives many quotations from protestant writings to the effect that evil princes are to be deposed, and that even a private man may kill a tyrant. But the most telling feature of the book is his account of the extent to which both classes and the more general assemblies had been actually held, and of the views and policies approved by them. Quoting from documents and from the statements of those examined in court, he compels belief, and is still, indeed, our principal source for knowledge of the growth and nature of the presbyterian movement under Elizabeth. Though he admits that the dissidents tried to keep within the law, he makes it plain beyond contradiction that their intent was to overthrow episcopacy and the Prayer Book. His evidence is not conjecture but quotation; it proves that there had not only been talk but definite action to try to set up the discipline quietly and surreptitiously.

Bancroft was unquestionably successful in revealing the danger of the presbyterian movement to the existing forms of church and state. He devoted comparatively little attention to the deeper question whether, despite such dangers, the presbyterian movement might not be right, according to the divine will as discernible in Scripture. Moreover, his whole style of writing was provocative rather than placatory. Already another defence of the Anglican position, at once more profound, more conciliatory, less involved in the circumstances of the day and so of more permanent interest, was in the making. Richard Hooker was busy with his *Laws of the Ecclesiastical Polity*. He had resigned the Mastership of the Temple in July 1591 on his appointment to a country living in Wiltshire. He was never resident in his new parish, as Professor Sisson has shown in his *Judicious Marriage of Mr. Hooker*; he remained in London at the house of his father-in-law. Almost certainly the purpose of the arrangement was not to give him rural peace but to free him from the contentious atmosphere and the routine duties of the Temple, that he might devote himself to his writing. It was not until 1595 that he left London for another country living near Canterbury to which the Archbishop presented him.

Professor Sisson has also shown that the generally accepted view, drawn from Walton's *Life*, of the genesis of the *Ecclesiastical Polity* must largely be abandoned. It was not the work of a lonely scholar, buried in the country; it was written in the heart of London, where its author could draw on the help and advice of his friends. In particular, Edwin Sandys, son of the Archbishop, a trained lawyer and a Member of Parliament, was closely interested, as was George Cranmer, another old friend. Their annotations to the Sixth Book still survive to show how actively they helped. Moreover, in the Dedication of the Fifth Book, Hooker speaks of the "long-continued and more than ordinary favour" he had enjoyed from the Archbishop, which confirms Sisson's suggestion that Whitgift had known of the project from the beginning—"the book had his blessing, as it surely had the benefit of his counsel". It was, after all, a continuation and an enrichment of the Archbishop's own controversial work. He might will be content to leave it—and encourage it—in the hands of a writer so skilled and temperate as Hooker had shown himself to be in his controversy with Travers. The work was thus no lone and secret venture; it was from the first favoured by Hooker's friends, and backed by the Primate.

The first four books were issued separately. They dealt, says Hooker, with "generalities of the cause in question" and so could appear as an introduction to the treatment of particulars which was to follow. There was, however, another and a pressing reason for this partial publication, as Sisson has shown. At first, Hooker had difficulty in finding a printer : he was told that such works were not saleable. It looks as though the market was overstocked with ponderous tomes of theology. Only when Sandys undertook the charges was a contract for publication signed on January 26, 1593. Then all was done with remarkable speed. On January 29 the book, already approved by the Archbishop, was duly entered on the Stationers' Register; on March 13, Hooker was able to send a copy of it to Burghley. On that very day, in the Commons, Sandys was insisting that Brownists and Barrowists should be made liable to punishment under the bill to deal with sectaries. The next day, the bill was delivered to Burghley to be considered in committee. Such synchronisation can hardly have been accidental. The first four books must have been hurried through the press to be ready for just such an occasion. Sandys, the Member of Parliament and man of affairs, had seen to it; Whitgift gave his approval with instant alacrity. For the Fifth Book, dealing with the detailed criticism by puritans of the Prayer Book and Church organization, there was no such hurry. It did not appear till 1597. The last three books, left incomplete when Hooker died in 1600, were not published till much later.

The *Ecclesiastical Polity* made an immediate impression far beyond mere Anglican circles; it is the chief literary outcome of the Elizabethan disputes to have living value except for the historian; it was so powerful that no serious attempt was made to answer it. Its most striking feature is perhaps neither the "judicious" weighing of arguments nor the massive learning, impressive though they are, but the general tone, so different from that normally prevalent. In his controversy with Travers, Hooker had managed to preserve seemliness; he still did so. Contemporary argument largely consisted of text-slinging and bickering over details and the possible implications of Scripture. Hooker stood out as one who was not just trying to make debating points but was passionately and majestically seeking truth. He was striving to persuade his opponents to think again, and could claim quite truthfully that his "endeavour is not so much to overthrow them with whom we contend as to yield them just and reasonable causes of those things, which, for want of due consideration heretofore, they misconceived". He had every reason to know that it was "not easy to speak to the contentation of minds exulcerated in themselves" and always ready to find fault. Repeatedly he warns against the dangers of such a spirit. "Better a great deal to be like unto those heretics which do nothing else but pray than those which do nothing else but quarrel." "Suspense of judgment and exercise of charity were safer and seemlier for Christian men than the hot pursuit of those controversies, wherein they that are most fervent to dispute be not always the most able to determine." He could have matched them in abuse had he so desired, but he had no wish to fan the flames. "Our answer to their reasons is no; to their scoffs nothing."

Hooker's first aim was to liberate the whole controversy from an almost suffocating biblicalism into a more generous breathing-space. Cartwright had maintained that "the word of God directeth a man in all his actions", even (unhappily) to the "taking up of a rush or straw". For every action some biblical warrant was to be produced. Hooker insists that man has guidance outside Scripture which also expresses God's will and purpose—natural laws and human laws—inevitable if men are to live in societies; there was, too, the divinely given power of reason to direct man in the choice of what is good. Scripture did not supplant but presupposed such guidances. It might at times correct them in detail or reinforce them if need be, but they still remained—especially reason—as divine guides to men side by side with Scripture, though of course the latter had unchallengeable authority in matters of salvation where it spoke clearly and unmistakably. The trouble came from the inferences drawn by analogy and ingenuity when the Scriptures were not clear. Thus, of their discipline he wrote that the best that could be said was "that *some things* which they maintain, as far as *some men* can *probably conjecture*, do *seem* to have been out of Scripture *not absurdly* gathered". But much of their reasoning rested on passages torn out of their context, or on the breaking of Hooker's simple rule "that where a literal construction will stand, the farthest from the letter is commonly the worst". He would not tolerate the idea that some Scripture warrant, however forced, must be produced for every action. Where there is not clear direction, it is enough if actions be "framed according to the law of reason". His opponents argued "as if the way to be ripe in faith were to be raw in wit and judgment; as if reason were an enemy unto religion, childish simplicity the mother of ghostly and divine wisdom".

Once he had thus cleared the way, Hooker could go ahead. He had little difficulty in showing that in many things, even ecclesiastical, there was in fact no exact Scripture guidance. The assumption that there must be a complete pattern in the Bible for church organization was only an assumption, not borne out by the evidence. Actually there was no such pattern in Scripture. Thus, though of course there must be church government, it need not be the same everywhere, just as, though all men needed language, they did not all have to have the same one. (Later on, however, he does insist that the three orders in the church go back to Apostolic times and, in fact, "had their beginning from Christ and his blessed Apostles themselves".) He effectively quotes Calvin in support of variety of rites, and deals fully with the common puritan assumption that anything taken from Rome must by that mere fact be wrong. Despite her faults, Rome is still part of the visible church. "With Rome we dare not communicate concerning sundry her gross and grievous abominations, yet touching those main parts of Christian truth wherein they constantly still persist, we gladly acknowledge them to be of the family of Jesus Christ", and pray for her reformation. Thus it is entirely right to continue such of her customs as reason approves if they are not against Scripture. To abolish at one sweep all her customs was dangerous : "the change of laws, especially concerning matters of religion, must be warily proceeded in."

In this wise, charitable, reasonable spirit Hooker comes later, in the Fifth Book, to the consideration of "particulars"—all the objections the puritans had raised against the Prayer Book and government of the English Church. He insists that here, too, reason must play its part, and experience. For "sharp and subtile discourses . . . laid in the balance with that which the habit of sound experience plainly delivereth" are "overweighed". Some external ceremonies are desirable—they may truly help devotion; certainly they are found to be useful in civil spheres. Traditions, too— "ordinances made in the prime of Christian religion, established with that authority which Christ hath left to his church for matters indifferent"—deserve careful consideration. It is all so reasonable, so peaceful, so quiet and patient, except where he has to deal with mere contentiousness, "the secret pernicious and pestilent conceit that the greatest perfection of a Christian man doth consist in discovery of other men's faults". He lays bare the danger of complete individualism that lies in such a spirit, and warns against the excessive valuation of sermons.

The *Ecclesiastical Polity* represents the crowning victory of Whitgift's campaign, raising the issues out of a mire of petty querulousness to a high level of reverence, toleration, humility. If a commander may be judged by the officers he chooses, Whitgift comes well out of the test by his choice of such assistants as vigorous Bancroft and "judicious" Hooker, and his active support of their work. But he had other things to do in those uneasy times. Despite the defeat of the Armada, the Council was continually alarmed by threats of invasion from Spain till the end of the reign. Nor was the alarm so baseless as it may now seem : in 1596 and 1597 Spanish fleets did actually sail to attack and were only prevented by storms : later on, there was a Spanish landing in Ireland. In the circumstances, it was only wise to keep strict watch on recusants, seminary priests and Jesuits. Of course, not all recusants were traitors : some affirmed that they would fight for the Queen against invaders, others refused to answer when the question was put to them, but some actually declared that they would fight for the Pope's cause. We can hardly call their treatment harsh in time of war and threatened invasion.

Normally either the courts of law or the Ecclesiastical Commission would deal with such cases; if the latter, Whitgift at its head was much concerned, especially in the trial of seminarists and Jesuits; and in keeping Burghley informed. He had, too, special responsibilities put on him by the Council. Kent, because of its proximity to the Continent, was particularly vulnerable; in 1593, therefore, he and the officials of his diocese were ordered to take special measures to search out recusant wives and especially, in the larger households, servants—for visiting priests were often concealed as such. There was to be careful enquiry throughout the diocese by curates and churchwardens. Again, when recusants at Broughton Castle were to be released on bail in 1590, it was the Archbishop whom they were to satisfy as to their places of residence. All this was both tiresome and onerous and it put a good deal of responsibility on the Archbishop : there were many who were very ready to blame him if things went wrong.

Though thus kept busy with the enemies of the Church of England on either side, Whitgift was also tireless to support it still by positive measures, to make it what he thought it ought to be. In 1591, alarmed by "the dissoluteness in manners and ignorance in the common sort", he wrote to the bishops of his province to press on their clergy the duty of catechizing the children in their parishes with the Shorter Catechism on Sunday afternoons, preferably in the presence of their parents who may thereby "take comfort and instruction also". Only those children who can say the Catechism are to be presented for Confirmation. Further, he urges the bishops themselves to be eager to confirm children at every opportunity. He was worried by the neglect of Confirmation. Just as he was always pressing for higher clerical standards, so he wished for an instructed and serious laity. "This ancient and laudable ceremony of confirming children, in respect of a carefulness in fathers to have their children instructed . . . hath heretofore wrought much good where it was used." Whitgift was sure that the neglect of it, and of the preparation for it, was the loss of a great opportunity.

His concern for the condition of the clergy came out very clearly prior to the Parliament of 1593. To be ready for any attacks which might be made there, he wrote to the bishops demanding an exact account of all the clergy in their dioceses—names, degrees, learning, conversation : whether they were preachers or not; which of them had actually been admitted by the bishops themselves; what clergy they had deprived for "insufficiency and lewdness of life". It was a serious attempt to take stock not only of the clergy but of the whole episcopal government. Moreover, Whitgift required all this, he asserted, at the Queen's "express pleasure and command". That, no doubt, was true.

She had assured Parliament that she would see to such things and she wanted now to know what the position was. In the Parliament Sir Robert Cecil was able to refer to her charge to the Archbishop as proof that she had taken care to redress what things were amiss in the church. But there can be no doubt that Whitgift welcomed the chance of making such a survey backed by the authority of the royal command.

No less significant was his choice of Lancelot Andrewes as preacher for the opening of Convocation in 1593. He was already well known to the Archbishop and was, indeed, now one of his chaplains. Whitgift must have guessed the kind of sermon he would preach. It was typical of the devout man who later on was twice to refuse a bishopric because of conditions which would have permanently impoverished the sees : he was not prepared to purchase personal advancement at such a price. His sermon was an urgent exhortation to his hearers to take heed unto their flocks who, even if they had not golden fleeces, had yet souls of gold. The moral earnestness of the sermon, its lively sense of clerical responsibility, are almost reminiscent of Latimer. The choice of such a preacher by Whitgift was entirely characteristic.

In 1594 also—again under direction from the Queen —he turned his attention to another cause of discontent : the ecclesiastical courts. These had long been a source of irritation : even before the break with Rome under Henry there had been complaints of them. But they had survived the breach, and still dealt not only with strictly spiritual or moral issues, but with probation of wills, matrimonial causes, questions of tithe, libels, as well as sex misdemeanours. They were dilatory, they were expensive in the matter of fees, they at times caused great offence by the use of excommunication for quite trivial matters. Often those who presided were laymen with no claim to any spiritual function; they were simply lawyers. And there were a great many such courts, not only provincial and diocesan, but archidiaconal. They were violently and justly resented : it was not only puritans who complained. So Whitgift set himself to find out what was really going on by a searching enquiry—whether the officers themselves presided in their courts or nominated agents, how many advocates and underlings were engaged about the courts, what "fees, rewards and wages" had been paid, what "injuries, extortions, oppressions and grievous exactions" had occurred. It was an honest attempt by the Queen and Archbishop to obtain a view of the whole picture of a part of the ecclesiastical system which was highly unpopular. The outcome of it we are not told; but the fact that such an enquiry was being made can scarcely have failed to have some salutary effect.

About now, too, Whitgift was driven to take up the cudgels against Beza, who was in an awkward position. As Calvin's successor in Geneva, he was an ardent believer in presbyteries; like Calvin, he was often approached for help by the English puritans. On the other hand, he did not wish to quarrel with Whitgift, whom he addressed with all the terms of respect due to his office. He was at last, however, provoked into indiscretion. Hadrian Saravia, a man of Spanish origin, after holding office as a pastor in the French church, had fled to England, where he won the patronage of Burghley and Whitgift. He was presented soon to a living and later to several prebends, without ever being ordained, so far as can be discovered, according to the Prayer Book rite. He became a close friend of Whitgift and of Hooker. In 1590 he published a book about the ministry which insisted that episcopacy was both primitive and scriptural. Beza was annoyed (naturally, in view of Saravia's earlier pastorate) and wrote a reply, only to be answered in turn by Saravia. Then Beza complained to Whitgift, who sent him an impressive and quite firm rejoinder. He recalled the times when the puritans had been encouraged from Geneva in their disturbing efforts; pointed out that if Saravia was attacked, it was but natural that he should defend himself; insisted that "the episcopal degree is an institution apostolical and divine; and so always hath been held by a continued course of times from the Apostles to this very age of ours". With an apology if he has spoken vehemently, he none the less declares his fervent wish that "every particular church would mind its own business, and not prescribe the laws of rites and the manner of government to others". It was a rebuke which Geneva amply deserved, and Beza more than Calvin.

Whitgift's love of orderliness, too, came out in his attention to the affairs of two hospitals in Canterbury where he sought to prevent abuses, and in directions to All Souls College, Oxford, of which he was Visitor. There he sought to check the Fellows from too much good living—private meals in their rooms and too many serving boys, instead of simply sharing the common meals. These, no doubt, were trivial matters of routine. But they illustrate the conscientious concern for order, discipline, correction of abuses, which affairs of church and state, however great, never deadened in the Archbishop.

Chapter Thirteen

Doctrinal Disputes
and Lambeth Articles

PROBABLY by temperament, certainly by the
course of his life, Whitgift was an administrator
rather than a speculative thinker. But in those contentious days he could not escape being involved in
doctrinal issues. There were varied interpretations of
the meaning of the statement, both in creed and
Articles, that Christ descended into hell. The
Edwardian Articles made it plain that this was to be
interpreted to mean in order to preach to the souls "in
prison or in Hell", according to the teaching of 1 Peter.
The expansion was omitted in the Elizabethan article,
and the statement left starkly that "he went down into
hell" (though the original Latin version simply said
"*ad inferos*"). In 1590, the Dean of Lincoln was de-
lated to the Archbishop by the Chapter of his cathedral for a sermon in which he had taught that, as Christ
took on him the sins of all, his descent into hell was
that he might endure the torments of hell as part of the
price of man's redemption. Whitgift, instinctively and
with wholesome common sense, was repelled by such
doctrine; examined the Dean, who promised not to
speak so again; and wrote to the Chapter to deal with
him brotherly and let the matter drop, for "there are
controversies enough in the Church of England".
Later on, he had arguments on the same point with
Broughton, a conceited and argumentative but learned
scholar, who insisted, and finally persuaded Whitgift,

that the descent should be thought of not as into hell the place of torment, but as into hades, the intermediate abode of departed souls whose ultimate lot might be joy or torment. Nowadays, it all seems too conjectural to be important. But Whitgift throughout appears in character—anxious for the peace of the church rather than for argument, shocked by the cruder forms which some of the continental teaching assumed, content to rest in that doctrine which the Scriptures expressly taught.

Much more important and troublesome was the controversy centred on the Calvinistic doctrine of predestination. Obsessed by the sense of God's almighty power, of His omniscience, and of a greatness which lifted Him above the rules of human justice, Calvin had pressed the doctrine of election with ruthless logic to repulsive extremes. Before the fall in Adam, even before men existed, God had predestined some to life and some to condemnation utterly regardless of any merit simply by His own inscrutable will and fiat. Calvin admitted that this theory of reprobation involved a "horrible decree", but not even his sense of that saved him from insisting on it, as logic seemed to him to require. The Anglican Articles of 1563 and 1571 were much more cautious. There is in them no mention at all of reprobation, and the omission was, we know, deliberate. Some of the exiles who returned from Switzerland in 1559 were not fully satisfied with the Edwardian Articles, specifically mentioning the importance of the doctrine of predestination in a declaration to the Queen. Thus the point cannot have been overlooked. Yet, when the Elizabethan Articles appeared, the only significant change from the Edwardian in that concerning predestination was the dropping of the clause which stressed that the divine decrees are unknown to us—a point dear to Calvin, and actually restored in the English Articles of 1571. There still remained the doctrine of the universal fall in Adam, involving all his posterity in an inclination to evil, though men are not described as a "mass of perdition", only as "very far gone from original righteousness". Their condition deserves "God's wrath and damnation", nor can any man "turn and prepare himself by his own natural strength and good works": there must be divine grace. Yet, somehow there is a lingering sense, however illogical, that man has some responsibility for his fate. The article specifically devoted to predestination treats explicitly only of "predestination to life"—the calling, adoption and sanctifying of those whom God by his secret counsel hath chosen in Christ. The emphasis is on God's mercy : the reverse is passed over silently. The whole topic is described, warningly, as very dangerous for "curious and carnal persons"; a paragraph at the end says that God's promises are to be received only as "generally" set forth in Scriptures—that is, for all men, not merely the elect; and insistence is laid on the doing of God's will as declared in the Scriptures.

Such teaching fell far short of what was desired by the zealous Calvinist who regarded each man's fate as unalterably fixed from eternity by divine decree; to whom good works had no value for salvation and for whom reprobation seemed to be as much an expression of the divine will as election to life. Such views, though deliberately not required by the Articles, were not flatly inconsistent with them, and quite soon those who held them began to teach as though they represented official Anglicanism. Thus a good deal of the criticism of Hooker by Travers rested, really, on such an interpretation of the teaching of the Articles. In Cambridge, in particular, many Heads of colleges seem to have thought that any lapse from pure Calvinism was heretical, their ablest champion being Dr. Whitaker, Master of St. John's and Regius Professor of Divinity. From about 1575, however, there began to emerge other views among the younger men, largely through the teaching of Peter Baro. Of French descent, he had been admitted to the ministry by Calvin himself in Geneva, a fact which did not make his criticisms of Calvin any the more palatable to Whitaker and the rest. Through the influence of Burghley, Baro was made Lady Margaret Professor in 1575; it is pleasant to think that his teaching may have been one of the influences which helped to mould Andrewes, then a coming man in Cambridge. It is certain that his lead affected many of the junior graduates who were thus brought to study the older Fathers and refused to regard Calvin as infallible. Obviously the situation was one which had to come to a head, though the explosion did not take place till 1595.

It was occasioned by a sermon from a young man, William Barrett, who rejected certain of Calvin's doctrines, and spoke violently against Calvin himself. He insisted that the cause of reprobation was actual sin, so rejecting the "horrible decree"; that no man could be securely certain that he would be saved, and that faith, even real faith, might be lost. Measures were at once taken against him by the Heads: he was prevented from taking his degree and made to read a recantation in St. Mary's. Both parties appealed to the Archbishop who, at first, despite his long-standing friendship with Whitaker, sympathised with Barrett. He did not approve of his strong language against Calvin, but did say that some of the views in his enforced recantation were "contrary to the doctrine holden and expressed by many sound and learned divines in the Church of England". No doubt he had in mind such men as Hooker, Andrewes—now one of his chaplains—and Saravia, who had written, apparently for the Archbishop, a critique of Barrett's recantation. Whitgift thought the authorities had acted harshly and hastily, and asserted that judgment in such matters was really his prerogative, not theirs.

The last point at once caused trouble, the Heads

insisting that they were only acting according to the University statutes and that the Archbishop had no authority in their affairs. To any such suggestion Whitgift was very sensitive : he replied with a firm letter insisting that he had the right, by virtue of the Commission for Ecclesiastical Causes, to deal with such matters in the University, as his predecessor Parker had done. That was a point about which he had no doubts. Nor was the University successful when it appealed to its Chancellor, Burghley, to protect its privileges. In self-defence, Whitgift pointed out to him that as he himself had procured the statutes, he really was likely to know what they meant, and that he had no intention of infringing them. Gradually, the Heads began to use more submissive language. Whitaker wrote to say that they had been "carried with desire to remove the great offence" Barrett had given to the University, and pleaded with the Archbishop "not to think unkindly of us that bear so dutifully affection to you". If they had acted beyond their statutes, they would acknowledge their mistake. Moreover, he did not now maintain, as at first he had blustered, that Barrett had offended against the Articles, but only "against the religion of our church, publicly received, and always held in her Majesty's reign"—which was precisely the point at issue. Even more submissively, the Heads presented their "humble suit" that "strict order may be taken, that no man presume . . . to maintain any opinion tending to innovation." With such an attitude Whitgift could be well content : at least his authority was admitted.

The original question, however, still remained to be settled. Barrett was examined before the Archbishop, and some of his views found to be unsatisfactory : a less onerous recantation was drawn up for him to read —though he does not seem ever to have done so. Further, a conference was called in London to consider the points raised. At this stage Baro took a hand by a sermon in Cambridge, delivered very modestly but with great courage. He maintained (if we may judge from a sermon a few weeks later) that God had created all men according to his own likeness in Adam and therefore for eternal life, that Christ's death was sufficient for all, and that the promises of God were to be "generally" understood, as in the Article. It was difficult to deny the biblical nature of such teaching : on the other hand, it was obviously flatly opposed to some of Calvin's views, and caused much resentment.

The conference took place at Lambeth in November 1595. The names of all who took part in it are not known for certain. Whitgift was there, with at any rate some other bishops; Whitaker and Tyndal, Dean of Ely, and others from Cambridge, Andrewes (apparently) and other divines. Whitaker and his friends proposed certain articles for acceptance; some alterations, seemingly small, were made in them, and the result was the so-called Lambeth Articles. The alterations, however, though trifling on the surface, were of substantial significance. What was originally a Calvinistic formula was in effect reduced to conformity with the official Anglican Articles, or very nearly so.

The opening statement looks ominous—God from eternity had predestined some to life and had reprobated some to condemnation. But that might be interpreted to mean no more than His resolve that believers should be saved and non-believers lost, as classes. So it was left : it does not have to be interpreted as fixing from eternity the fate of every individual, though that had doubtless been what was originally intended. After that, there is no more about reprobation. Those who are not predestined to life are condemned for "their own" sins : a deliberate addition to Whitaker's article, stressing a point which we know Whitgift felt strongly. Their fate was not the result of a divine fiat, but was deserved because of their sin. Other changes made it clear that the only predestination being treated was that "to life", and that it was due to the sole will of a benevolent God. Moreover, though in the elect faith never fails finally or totally, it is implied that some men who are not elect may have faith for a time, but then lose it—so there is no basis for the security which made some Calvinists so objectionable, and which Whitaker's article would have encouraged.

Much in the Lambeth Articles may cause disquiet to a modern reader; they draw the lines more definitely and firmly than the Thirty-nine. It is insisted that all men deserve condemnation for their sins; that it is not in their choice to win salvation, for which they must depend entirely on divine calling and grace; that God has fixed the number whom He will call, which cannot be increased or diminished. All that is still there : few in those days thought otherwise. But the most repulsive features of Calvinism were gone. Those who were to be condemned met their fate for their own sins not because of a "horrible decree"; so far as God interfered it was of sheer good will, to pick out some for salvation without their deserving it at all. That might not be strict justice, in the human sense; but it was at least merciful.

The Lambeth Articles thus were a check to the attempt to read a full Calvinistic doctrine into the Thirty-nine Articles—and for that check Whitgift deserves gratitude. He was also no doubt well satisfied that the University had come to heel in the matter of his authority. In the end, however, the Lambeth Articles never had any official confirmation as an expression of Anglicanism. Whitgift, in his covering letter to Cambridge, made it clear that they were not to be regarded as "laws and decrees", but as "private judgments" corresponding to the doctrine of the Church of England. Any contrary teaching should be checked, but "discretion and moderation" should be used in teaching the Articles agreed at Lambeth, and those who dissented should "not be of purpose stung or justly grieved". Though Hutton, Archbishop of York, expressly agreed with most of the Articles, they quickly fell into the background. The Queen heard of them, and had a letter sent to Whitgift to say that she "misliked much" that the Archbishop and the rest had allowed such points to be disputed, "being a matter tender and dangerous to weak ignorant minds". Whitgift, thus warned, wrote further to Cambridge that, though the Queen was persuaded of the truth of the propositions, yet the Articles should only be used privately and not published. Shortly afterwards, Whitaker died, and was succeeded as Professor by Overall, who was a friend of Baro. Baro himself was protected by his patron Burghley from the vengeance of the opposing Heads, but wisely did not seek re-election to his professorship. So the trouble died down. When in 1604 an attempt was made to gain official sanction for the Lambeth Articles, it was completely unsuccessful. In the matter of doctrine, as in the matter of ecclesiastical government, Whitgift had been successful in preventing the imposition of full Calvinism on the Church of England.

The anxieties of the watchful Archbishop did not end there. A careful eye had still to be kept on church property. The fully legalised claims of the state were bad enough. The wealthy see of Ely, for example, had been without a bishop since the death of Cox in 1581 (it was not filled until December 1598). The delay was due to the desire to make exchanges, highly profitable to the Crown, of royal and episcopal possessions, which was allowed by law during a vacancy. Thus Burghley wrote in 1595 to his son Robert, a Secretary of State, to warn him not to take further steps to fill the vacancies at Winchester and Durham, until full provision and assurance had been made for such "rents and amenities" as ought to be secured from them. And the concealers were still busy. The Parliament of 1597-8 found it necessary to pass an act confirming the right

of the Bishop of Norwich to certain monastic possessions actually conveyed to him by act of Parliament
under Henry VIII. They should, surely, have been
safe enough; but attempts were now made to seize
them as concealed ecclesiastical property really be-
longing to the Crown. Such matters must have troubled
the Archbishop, with his strong realisation of the
dangers of clerical poverty. We know that about now
he did recover for Eastbridge Hospital certain lands of
which it had been wrongfully deprived as concealed,
and secured another hospital from the depredations of
a powerful neighbour who was wrongly taking timber
which belonged to it.

A more general problem was presented by the growing number of "rogues, vagabonds and sturdy beggars".
It was partly due to soldiers and mariners discharged
from Elizabeth's forces, partly to a series of bad har-
vests which meant hard times even for the honest poor,
however hard-working. The situation was such that Parliament, in 1597–8, took strenuous measures, ordering
parishes to make provision for the poor by a levy, with
overseers to administer the proceeds, and providing for
the voluntary erection of hospitals for the poor. Provision was also made for the necessary relief of discharged
soldiers, though measures were passed against those
who falsely claimed to be such. For "rogues" and the
rest, houses of correction were to be erected. In 1601,
Parliament re-enforced some of these measures, and
actually discussed the desirability of limiting the number of ale-houses, chiefly, no doubt, because of the
amount of tippling, but partly because of the amount
of corn they used, a cause of grumbling at a time when
prices had swollen, and farmers were yet holding back
supplies for a still further rise. Whitgift was not one
who wore his heart on his sleeve, but he realised
strongly that here was a situation in which the church
had a clear duty to do something. In August 1596, and
again in December, he wrote to the bishops to stir up

their clergy to preach in support of the measures the
Queen had taken both to prevent further rise in prices
and to provide cheap corn for the poor. Farmers were
to be exhorted not to seek gain by the oppression of
their poor neighbours; the rich to use hospitality and
to eat sparingly, especially on fast days, so that what
was saved could be given to the needy—even the keeping of hounds was to be discouraged because of what
they ate. Servants should not be discharged to "shift
for themselves"; rather work should be found for the
needy, and alms increased. Clergy were to reside in
their livings and provide hospitality. His letters, indeed,
are full of practical hints of how the situation could
be eased. His own contribution was that by which he
is probably still best remembered—the erection of the
Hospital of the Holy Trinity and a free school at Croydon. The work began, under licence from the Queen,
in 1595 and was completed in 1599—"One of the most
notable monuments founded in these times", says
Strype. Provision was made for twenty-eight poor,
needy or impotent persons and as many more under
forty as could be afforded; a school house was built
and a dwelling for the master. For one who was not
wealthy, it was a munificent foundation, a generous
gesture and an example for others to follow. Though
it may have been due, as was nearly everything else he
did, to a high sense of duty, it was also very near his
heart. In his closing years he was a constant visitor to
it, "often dining at the hospital among his poor
brethren, as he called them". Had he known that posterity would chiefly cherish his memory because of it
and his school, he would have been well contented.

Whitgift's concern for the improvement of the
church where there were still faults continued un-
abated. Clergy who did not reach the required standard, and the abuses of clerical courts were the outstanding blemishes. The Parliament of 1597 was
allowed by the Queen "full liberty to reform some

abuses", though not, of course, to suggest alterations in the ministry or service of the church. In the end, an act was passed to deprive of benefit of clergy those who took part in the marriage, against their will, of widows, heiresses, etc., or robbed houses. Other bills, much discussed though not enacted, show the sort of practical abuses which provoked the laity. There was a great deal of indignation about irregular marriages which were facilitated by licences for marriage without banns. There were grumbles about the ecclesiastical courts, excessive fines, delays, and the oath *ex officio*.

Whitgift, thoroughly awake to all this, used the Convocation which met concurrently with Parliament to try to improve matters. He laid before the Lower House a long list of disorders—excessive apparel of ministers, neglect of their cathedral duties by prebendaries, disorderly marriages, divorces too easily pronounced, the too great number and ill behaviour of the officials of the courts. Thus impelled, Convocation passed a series of Constitutions which were confirmed by the Queen and promulgated under the great seal of the realm. There was renewed insistence that bishops should admit only suitable men to orders, or to livings. Precautions against abuse of marriage by licence were strengthened. New sections insisted that beneficed clergy should exercise hospitality: that cathedral clergy must preach in their turn; that divorce should not be rashly pronounced; that recusants and excommunicants should be publicly denounced; that registers should be properly kept. In particular, there was a long new section ordering the open display of fees which were customarily charged in the church courts from the beginning to the eighteenth year of the reign: they were not to be exceeded.

The Constitutions of 1597 show Whitgift's unremitting determination to deal with the shortcomings of the church. He was not content to leave it at that. In November he wrote to the bishops to complain that irregular marriages, without banns or in private houses, were still taking place; they must be stopped. In the same month also he sent round a serious rebuke to those bishops who had not carried out some of the things ordered in the Constitutions—a neglect, he said, "which argueth that you have not that vigilant care in executing other parts of the said constitutions, as you ought, and as her Majesty expecteth".

In the same year Whitgift did one further service to the church he so zealously safeguarded. With Burghley's support, he secured the nomination of Bancroft to the vacant bishopric of London. From the location of his office, no less than by ancient custom, the Bishop of London was second only to the Primate in the southern province. Bancroft had shown himself able, determined, vigorous and, above all, a convinced upholder of church order at it was. He was now placed in a position in which, with full weight and authority, he could support the ageing Archbishop.

Lapse of time did not dull vigilance. In 1599, Whitgift wrote severely to the Bishop of Peterborough who had not sent in a complete but only a partial list of fees chargeable in his diocese. In the Convocation of 1601 he returned to the attack. In the concurrent Parliament the strong puritan element brought forward measures to enforce Sabbath observance, to punish wilful absence from church on Sunday, to check blasphemous swearing, to control pluralities and against commissaries' and archdeacons' courts, as well as the bill against ale-houses. None of them reached the statute book, but they showed that the puritan spirit was still alive. To excessive sabbatarianism Whitgift was no friend—in 1599 he tried to put a stop to the circulation of books which pleaded for it. But he showed that he recognised the legitimacy of some of the other complaints by urging the assembled bishops to check the still prevalent abuses in the ecclesiastical courts—to see that they were not held too often, that men were not summoned to several courts for the same offence, that they were not tried merely on the motion of court officials. He urged, too, that the curates of non-residents should be able persons, properly paid, so as to lessen complaints about pluralities; and that licence to marry without banns should not be granted by any official other than the diocesan chancellor. A month or so later, he followed this up with a letter to the bishops, pointing out that the "multitudes of complaints" made in the last Parliament had even endangered the existence of the clerical courts, and pressing once more for a "careful and vigilant heed to the constitutions made in the former Convocation and confirmed by her most excellent Majesty". He added a list, again, of the abuses he thought most serious.

Such unremitting care compels admiration. The Archbishop was now a man of seventy; for years he had been anxious, slandered by his enemies, constantly on guard. Yet there is no sign of relaxation or flagging. Selfless dedication to the well-being of the church he loved was still as complete as in his early days in Cambridge.

Chapter Fourteen

Last Days of Whitgift

ON March 24, 1603, Queen Elizabeth died. She had been ill from early in the month. At first she was listless, lacking in vitality and liveliness, though, to the end, there was no sign of any mental failing. After a rally in the middle of the month, she grew worse, but refused to take to her bed. For three days and nights she lay on cushions in her privy chamber. Then, partly by persuasion and partly by force, she was put to bed. Unable now to speak, she managed, by signs, to make it clear that she wanted the Archbishop to come to her. He spoke of her faith and of the account she must soon have to make. With hand and eye she showed her understanding. The Archbishop prayed by her side for a long half-hour : when he was about to rise, she signalled to him to continue; and so it happened yet again. Thus she spent her last conscious hours in devotions with her "little black husband" as she used to call him : it was the last help her old friend and ally could give her. Afterwards she fell asleep and died quietly in the early morning.

It was the end of a partnership very fruitful for the Church of England. No doubt, she was not an easy woman to work with, and at times Whitgift must have found her difficult. But she was genuinely fond of him and had fewer serious differences from him than from most of those who were her chief officers and favourites. Possibly her motives throughout were political rather than religious, while Whitgift was solely concerned for the good of the church. But they were complementary to each other. She used her strength and her skill in the management of her subjects to protect the ecclesiastical settlement from attack or change. That alone would not have been enough. Under her protection, it was the zeal and constant devotion of the Archbishop which brought life and healing to a church which was in a sad condition of confusion at the beginning of the reign. In the last ten years there had been a marked change. The puritans were more or less quiescent; the recusants, for the most part, were loyal to the Queen though they were still not entirely trusted; above all, the church was in better heart, securing a much improved type of ordinand—men of higher education, whose loyalty to the church in which they had been born and bred was genuine, untouched by leanings either to Rome or Geneva, which they had never personally known. Both in learning and character, thanks to Whitgift's constant efforts, the clergy were of infinitely better standard. At the beginning of the reign only a minority were University graduates; the majority were so at the end.

Within eight hours of the Queen's death, James was proclaimed King in London. There were none of the difficulties which had for years been apprehended concerning the succession. None the less, it was an anxious time for the Archbishop. Despite the years of comparative peace and improvement, the settlement could not yet be regarded as secure. There were many Romanists in the country, secretly served by priests from abroad; there were many puritans, including rich and influential laymen as well as learned ministers. Though numbers cannot be exactly calculated, there was certainly plenty of tinder ready to take fire at a spark. Above all, the new King was very much an unknown quantity. He was, beyond question, learned. He had, too, acquired much knowledge of ecclesiastical arguments, and a good deal of skill in them. He was genuinely interested in such things—much more than Elizabeth had ever been. But what were his own personal preferences, or what would be his policy, was not at all clear. The precariousness of his position in Scotland, the constant tension of rival parties, had imposed on him a secretiveness and skill in management which effectually concealed what he wanted himself.

In fact, what he really wished for, above everything, was the throne of England. It never occurred to him that he would ascend it with such ease. Thus his policy had been to conciliate all parties and offend none so that he might succeed with the good will of all. In 1591 he wrote to Elizabeth on behalf of the imprisoned puritans. On the other hand, before her death, he wrote to a leading catholic noble that he would not persecute any catholics who were quiet and outwardly obedient. But it was not mere policy, much less hypocrisy. He had seen enough of quarrels and presecution to wish for tolerance and conciliation. For the simple puritan and the loyal recusant he had respect and liking. What he could not bear was the hectoring presbyterian minister or the scheming Roman priest, each of whom almost equally threatened the royal supremacy so dear to his heart. No title could have summed up the part he wished to play better than that of "Supreme Governor" of the church.

That, however, was not at first obvious to contemporaries. It is true that he gave a friendly answer to the Dean of Canterbury, Whitgift's emissary to assure him of the loyalty of the Church of England and to seek his protection for it. He would, he said, uphold the government of the late Queen. But, equally, on his way to London, he received graciously the puritans who presented their Millenary Petition; the loyal recusants, too, were led to expect milder treatment, if only by the remission of fines. It may well all have been due to a genuine spirit of generous toleration as much as to mere policy. In those days of unsparing partisanship, however, it could not so be seen; it was enigmatic and suspect.

Whitgift was worried. He at once took steps to enable him to give a full account of the condition of the church. In May he wrote to the bishops to supply him with information of the names and degrees of all preachers, by whom they were licensed to preach and where they lived. On June 30 he sought for fuller particulars—the number of communicants in each parish, and of recusants and non-communicants; the names of pluralists in each diocese, the number of impropriated livings and the salaries of the curates who served them, the name of the patron of each benefice. When the returns came in, they showed that there had been an obvious increase of recusancy since James's accession, clearly due to the hope of more lenient treatment. Even so, it has been calculated that, on average, there were fewer than one recusant for each parish against more than 250 communicants. Still, recusancy looked like a growing danger. And, on the other side, the puritans were busy organizing once more and arranging for a flood of petitions.

In the end both parties overplayed their hands. A couple of obscure but easily detected Romanist plots in 1603, one headed by William Watson, the other by Lord Cobham, were followed by a proclamation in February 1604 ordering all Jesuits, seminarists and other priests to depart the realm before March 19. The King, indeed, did try to reach a *modus vivendi* with the papacy; but when the attempt failed, he took firm measures. Henceforward there was no fear of over-indulgence to Romanists. Meantime, the puritan schemers, thinking they had won the King's ear by the Millenary Petition, had drawn up a model form of petition to be submitted by large numbers of (supposedly) independent suppliants.

The Millenary Petition itself was, on the surface, surprisingly moderate. It did not suggest any "dissolution of the state ecclesiastical" but only the "redress of divers abuses of the church". The old objections to the Prayer Book were once more paraded—the signing with the cross and the interrogatories of sponsors at baptism; confirmation; the ring at marriage; cap and surplice and the rest. There were requests that only able and sufficient men should be admitted to the ministry and non-residence forbidden; that pluralism should be stopped, and impropriations taken away from bishops and colleges—and partly even from private holders—to be used for the support of preaching ministers; for the reform of procedure in the church courts, for a more sparing use of the oath *ex officio*, and of excommunication for slight reasons. There was no suggestion of revolutionary measures, only of reform of abuses which could be corrected without interfering with fundamentals. Now, James wished for the reform of abuses and was perhaps touched by the humble tone of the address. He even went so far as to write to the two Universities to say that he would devote all royal impropriations to the improvement of livings and hoped that the Universities would do the same.

Whitgift had an inkling of what was happening. If the dating of the letters is to be trusted, he wrote to the King the day before the royal letter to the Universities, to urge that the impropriations were already being properly used "for the general necessities of the whole church" and that to withdraw them from the Universities would lead to the overthrow of learning. Both Universities condemned the Petition. Oxford drew up a full reply, rejecting the remedies proposed by the puritans, showing the practical difficulties they would cause and arguing that the real purpose of the petition was, in the end, the "setting up of a presbytery in every parish". When the King arrived in London, both Whitgift and Bancroft, who now comes increasingly to the front, had interviews with him. After that, there was no more talk of impropriations being re-assigned, and the King was no longer so gracious to the puritans. He had become more fully instructed as to the situation by Bancroft, who had a thorough knowledge and experience of puritan tactics.

When the stream of petitions began to pour in, according to the puritan plan, the King was thus fully prepared to be suspicious. The result was a strongly worded royal proclamation on October 24. The King declared that, since he understood the form and frame of the church, he found both the constitution and doctrine "agreeable to God's word and near to the condition of the primitive church". He realised, how-ever, that human imperfections might blemish even a well-constituted church; he had therefore ordered a meeting to consider complaints he had received point-ing out abuses. But he now found that his intention had been misunderstood by men "whose heat tendeth rather to combustion than to reformation"; there were invectives against the authority and courts of the church, "subscriptions of multitudes of vulgar persons to supplications", and the like. Such courses were unlawful and savoured of "tumult, sedition and violence". If, at the proposed meeting, any abuses should be proved, they would be lawfully corrected "by advice of our council, or in our high court of parliament, or by convocation of our clergy". Two days later the King wrote to Whitgift that he did not mean to give way to "unquiet persons" and that con-formity should be enforced. "To my comfort" the Archbishop wrote in December, "I am assured by his Majesty's letters writ to me, that they have not much prevailed. . . . I have not all this while been idle, nor greatly quiet in mind. For who can promise himself rest among so many vipers?"

To an impartial reader, the royal proclamation should have made the King's intentions quite clear. There was to be no change in essentials; proved abuses would be corrected by orderly process. The puritans, however, were not impartial. They were elated that they were to meet the bishops in argument on equal terms—a thing Elizabeth had never allowed—and seem to have thought that principles as well as details were to be reviewed. They were sadly disillusioned in the event. In fact, the two sides were never set in full debate one against the other. The conference met at Hampton Court in January 1604. On the first day the bishops (nine in number) with the six deans present were summoned to appear before King and Council, the puritan spokesmen (four, five or six uncertain) being left outside. The King put to the bishops certain points in the Prayer Book—absolution, the nature and use of Confirmation, private baptism and some others —which seemed to him to call for comment or explanation. He spoke of what he thought to be the excessive use of excommunication for small matters. Whitgift replied firmly, asserting that in church the minister only pronounced an absolution in general, that Confirmation was an ancient and valuable rite, and that it was not intended that private baptism should be administered by women or lay persons. After long discussion, King and bishops agreed on practically all points, and James instructed them to draw up in due form the changes and explanations which should be made.

After a day's interval, the King interviewed the puritans. It was not the stately debate they had expected. Whitgift and most of the bishops were not present, only Bancroft and one other. The meeting was not happy for the puritans. At the outset, the King told them that he proposed to make no innovations. Bancroft was allowed to break into their arguments. James did not restrain him, and treated the puritans with a good deal of sharpness. He agreed that there should be some expansion of the Catechism, and a new English version of the Bible, a project he had long favoured.

Guided by Bancroft, he rejected the proposal that the
Lambeth Articles should be included in the Articles of
Religion, declared himself in favour of episcopal confirmation, and assured the puritans that the bishops
were just as eager for a learned ministry as they were.
Proposals that the prophesyings should be renewed,
and that bishops should be assisted in their decisions
by learned presbyters greatly roused him. "When I
mean to live under a presbytery, I will go unto Scotland again", he said, and reminded them what had
happened there when Knox was their leader. "No
bishop, no King", he remarked, and ended, "if this be
all that they have to say, I shall make them conform
themselves."

Two days later was the last meeting of the Conference. First of all Whitgift presented to the King, in
the presence of the chief ecclesiastical judges, the suggested changes, prepared according to the King's instructions. The King approved them. There was a discussion about the powers and size of the Ecclesiastical
Commission, which Whitgift defended to the satisfaction of the King, who also approved the *ex officio*
oath. Then, and only then, the puritan spokesmen were
admitted, supported by some thirty other leading puritans. They were not allowed to argue. The King had
read out to them the points on which he had decided
to take action, and urged them to try by example and
persuasion to win over their fellows to conformity. One
concession James did make—for a time, the surplice
and crossing at baptism were not to be pressed in
Lancashire. When a similar concession was asked for
Suffolk it was refused, with acrimony.

The most important outcome of the Conference was,
of course, the Authorised Version of 1611. For this, at
least, James deserves full credit. From the first he was
zealous for it. He himself suggested the method to be
followed and set out elaborate instructions for the
translators to prevent unfamiliar innovations in word-

ing and to safeguard the meaning of the original against partisan glosses and notes. The translators, who included known puritans, were chosen for their scholarship alone, not their views. Fifty-four in number, they worked in six groups, with ample provision for criticism and correction of each section. The whole was revised by a committee of six and finally by Bishop Bilson and Miles Smith. The King urged on the bishops the duty of rewarding the translators by preferment. Their greater reward was to have enriched, for centuries to come, English language, English character, essential English life, with a treasure beyond price.

Apart from the Authorised Version, the only notable results of the Conference were a section on sacraments added to the Catechism, and some changes in the rubrics in the Prayer Book, especially about Confirmation and Private Baptism. The disappointment of the puritans was proportionate to the high hopes they had cherished beforehand. On the King, the result was to confirm him, despite the moderation of the Millenary Petition, in the suspicions Bancroft had sowed about puritan aims, methods and unreasonableness. Otherwise, he could scarcely have written as he did, just after the Conference, "We have kept such a revel with the Puritans here this two days, as was never heard the like; where I have peppered them as soundly as ye have done the Papists." Few things could be more revealing of the King's lack of sympathy with them all along. For all their faults, the puritans were sincere, and many of them were learned. They deserved more considerate treatment than abuse and scorn, if they were to be argued with at all. A layman who was present says the bishops declared that "the king spoke by the power of inspiration," but adds that "the spirit was rather foul-mouthed."

Bancroft had been the main speaker in such argument as had taken place, but Whitgift also had done his part, defending the Commission, and agreeing with the King on desirable alterations. It was his last great service to the church. He was already an old man, and had recently been ill with "my old disease, the jaundice" Towards the end of February, he caught a chill when crossing the river in his barge to Fulham. Nothing daunted, he and the Bishop of London had a long conference with the King at Whitehall on the following Sunday. After it he had a seizure which paralysed him on one side and impaired his speech. The King showed much concern and visited him at Lambeth, but all that could be understood of the Archbishop's speaking was "*Pro Ecclesia Dei*". On Wednesday, February 29, 1604, he died. He was buried, suitably enough, in the parish church at Croydon, near his beloved hospital, with due solemnity on March 27. Between his death and his burial, there was a royal proclamation confirming the results of the Hampton Court Conference and ordering conformity to the Prayer Book. It is due to his dedicated life to hope that, before he died, Whitgift knew that it was to come; that at least he lived long enough to be assured that the King would firmly uphold the Church of England against both Romanists and puritans.

"He was of a middle stature, of a grave countenance and brown complexion, black hair and eyes; he wore his beard neither long nor thick." So wrote one who knew him well. He was not a man to fire romantic imagination. It would be wrong to suggest that his friends did not feel affection for him; evidently the Queen liked him, and Burghley and many others. Still, in the main, respect rather than love is the response he won and wins. Though said to have had a quick temper, the over-all impression is of a man whose life was controlled and surrendered entirely to the service of the church, and in whom emotions were allowed little play. It is true that he was described as cheerful and affable, yet it is, somehow, difficult to think of him as heartily enjoying a joke, just as it is impossible to find him querulous (as Parker was) at the burdens the Queen put upon him. It is odd that he seems never to have been moved to visit Cambridge once he left it for Worcester, despite his interest in the University and his many friends there. But he did win respect from all those who had personal dealings with him, save the embittered puritans. Even they, at their most violent, could do little more than call him pope or tyrant or persecutor. But, as he wrote to Burghley, he had taken upon him "the defence of the religion and rites of this church. . . . It is more than strange that a man in my place, dealing with so good warrantise as I do, should be so hardly used, and for not yielding be counted wilful. But *vincit qui patitur.*" And so, to a great extent, he did. He bore no grudges and forbore to press the puritans as soon as their conduct allowed him to do so. The degree to which they had quieted down by the end of the reign of Elizabeth must surely be attributed not only to the strong measures against them in 1591–3, but also to the fact that they had not been harried afterwards. Shortly after his death, the Earl of Salisbury declared that there was nothing more to be feared in his government (especially towards the end) than his "mildness and clemency". The greatest of his contemporaries who knew him best would not have recognised in him Macaulay's "narrow-minded, mean and tyrannical priest".

It is a surprise—perhaps the only one he offers—to find that he lived in considerable splendour, with a great number of retainers. When he visited Canterbury, his own attendants might number ten score and be swollen by the neighbouring gentry to a crowd of eight hundred. He kept an armoury capable of equipping a hundred foot soldiers and fifty horse. His hospitality was lavish; he often feasted the clergy and gentry of his diocese; and at Christmas time kept open house for strangers. On great occasions he was served "upon the knee", not out of pride, but "for the upholding of the state that belonged unto his place". Once or more each year he entertained the Queen—much to her satisfaction. His personal preference, however, was to steal away and sup with the poor brethren in his hospital at Croydon.

He used his position to forward two causes very near his heart—education and the assistance of those in need. He kept about him numbers of young men for instruction in mathematics and "sundry arts and languages", personally took part in their training, giving them allowances and securing preferments for them. It was what might justly be "accounted a little academy and in some respects superior and more profitable", says Paule. He also maintained some students at the University. He was no less solicitous for those who needed help. Twice a day he gave audience to suitors, whom his officers were told to entertain courteously, and he was always ready to help the destitute with money or goods or by a gift of tools for their trade. His hospital and school at Croydon simply summarized and crowned what were constant activities.

Though fully conscious of the dignity and duties of his office, Whitgift was without personal ambition or love of power for its own sake. He refused the Chancellorship of Oxford, and the Lord Chancellorship of the realm. It is even said that he withdrew from meetings of the Council if he found that there was no business to be done which touched on church affairs. Nor did he use his position to found a family or accumulate a fortune. His income he spent on what he conceived to be the duties of his post; what he had over he used for his Croydon foundations. The only legacies mentioned are gifts of books and manuscripts to Cambridge colleges.

The Elizabethan bishops were an abler and more conscientious body of men than has sometimes been supposed, but on any estimate Whitgift stands out preeminent among them—"a man born for the benefit of his country and the good of his church " says Strype. His patience, persistence, strength, understanding, and, perhaps, above all, integrity were invaluable. "Happy surely was it for that crazy state of the Church (for so it was at this Archbishop's first coming and long after) not to meet with too rough and boisterous a physician." So Sir George Paule, and for once in a way the estimate of a professional eulogist may be endorsed. The Caroline divines were in no small measure the fruit of Whitgift's untiring labours to provide a better sort of ministry. That the church acquired the vitality and drew to itself the loyal devotion which enabled it to emerge triumphantly from the attacks of the Commonwealth period was largely the result of Whitgift's work and of the men he encouraged and inspired.

Books for Further Reading

Life of Whitgift. Sir George Paule.

Works of Whitgift. Ed. J. Ayre (Parker Society).

Strype, Annals, Life of Whitgift, and of Grindal.

History of the Church of England in the reigns of Elizabeth and James I. W. H. Frere.

Puritan Manifestoes. W. H. Frere and C. E. Douglas.

Tudor Puritanism. M. M. Knappen.

Thomas Cartwright and Elizabethan Puritanism. A. F. Scott-Pearson.

The Presbyterian Movement in the Reign of Queen Elizabeth. R. G. Usher.

The Reconstruction of the English Church. R. G. Usher.

King James VI and I. D. H. Willson.

Index

A

B

C

INDEX

P

R

S